Trout etcetera

Brian Clarke

Trout etcetera

Illustrations by Michael J. Loates

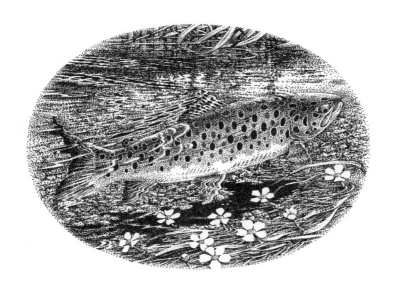

A & C Black · London

First published 1996 by
A & C Black (Publishers) Ltd
35 Bedford Row, London WC1R 4JH

Text copyright © 1996 by Brian Clarke
Illustrations copyright © 1996 by Michael J. Loates

ISBN 0 7136 4558 X

A CIP catalogue record for this book is available from the
British Library.

Typeset in 10½ on 13pt Galliard
Printed and bound in Great Britain by
Printed by The Lavenham Press Ltd., Lavenham, Suffolk, England

Dedication

For Anne,
my wife and dearest friend

Contents

Introduction

This book contains some of the pieces I have published on angling and angling matters over recent years. They are drawn from a range of sources. The name of the newspaper, magazine or book in which each originally appeared is given, where relevant, as is the date of publication. I have also included a number of pieces not previously published which, for one reason or another, I wished to appear here. These pieces are, of course, those which are uncredited and undated.

In the main, each piece has been used as originally published, except that here and there I have put back minor cuts and changes made for reasons of space or house style; and I have from time to time made a clarification or two, or added a discussion point or two, where that has seemed to add value.

The pieces are not grouped or ordered in any particular way. I dip into collections like this as though into a bran tub and I do not deceive myself that my own golden words will be treated differently by others. The only exceptions are the placings of the first piece and the last, which seemed to me to form natural bookends.

Acknowledgements

I am grateful to the following for their permission to use material originally commissioned by them: The Editors of *The Times, The Sunday Times, The Guardian* and *The Field*; to Merlin Unwin for permission to reprint my essay 'Lost Fish' from *The One That Got Away*; to B.T. Batsford for permission to reprint 'Trout in the Green-hazed Tunnel' from *West Country Fly Fishing*; to Swan Hill Press for permission to reproduce 'A Glass-case Trout' from *Lessons from the Fish*; and to the Flyfishers' Club and the Salmon and Trout Association.

Brian Clarke,
June 1996.

First Cast

The close season lasts so long. Three weeks in and we feel perhaps yes, this is not so bad. Five or six weeks in – well, we are getting by, we are coping better this year. With three fishless months behind and three more to go, time is dragging. By January we are restless and by February, pent up. Will it never end? Never?

That is the way my close seasons go, anyway. By the time spring comes and the air warms and the first silken leaves are beginning to unfurl, I cannot wait. Especially if, as sometimes happens, I have a hurt inside and a score to settle. FROM *The Times*, May 18, 1993.

First day back on the river, first day of the new season and my hurrying footsteps can slow. He is still there. After all this time he is still there. Even from here, looking downstream and across, I can see him rising beneath the far bank: see the soft crinklings of light when he sips down a fly.

It will have to be the same approach: into the water downstream of the alder, across the river as far as I can wade and then that slow, uncertain inching upstream to within casting distance again. If I approach from here I will be in full view; if I approach him from anywhere other than downstream there has to be a risk.

I make a detour over the meadow on my own bank, crawl on my hands and knees to the alder and slip into the water. A coot explodes from the rushes and runs full-tilt across the surface, leaving a linked chain of rings spreading out. A vole nibbling weed pauses and peers, senses danger or my tension and is gone with a plop.

The world closes in. The songs of the lark and the cuckoo fade. The purple-hazed woods across the valley, the butter-cupped fields all around, dissolve to soft focus. I am alone with the fish, locked onto it, fused to it. Little by little I make my way across and then up.

I move so as to come as close in behind him as I can. Every trout has a blind spot behind it because of the way its eyes are angled slightly towards the front. Positioned that way, the fish gets the binocular vision that any predator needs. But there is a price to pay. This price.

I know the problems well, have thought them through time and time over. They have not changed. The trout is in a narrow channel that a wide bed of weed forces into the bank. Midway between the weed and the bank a wooden post sticks up. The trout is just in front of this post, riding the current, drifting idly to his left and his right, picking out flies from the concentrated stream of food that the weedbed funnels in. Getting my fly into that yard-wide channel, catching neither the weedbed nor the bank and avoiding the post, is the first problem.

The second problem is the other post. It does not break the surface and you would never know it was there. But I do. It is just downstream from the first post where the trout is lying. It was around the second post that he broke me before: on my last cast of my last day, last season.

I am right behind him, now; probably not in his blind spot but close to it, somewhere on the periphery of his vision, out from his flank about 15 yards behind. I edge forward another yard or two. I can probably reach him from here.

Up he comes again, this time sliding so far to his right that he moves big water. I mark his position precisely, hold myself ready and unhitch the fly. The water toys with the light, slipping it here, sliding it there. A frond of weed moves in sensuous curves. The water eases and crinkles. I can hear his sipping through the silence I have made: the small noise he cannot help making because each time he sucks in a fly he sucks in some air as well.

There is his nose again, there is the sip, there are the rings. I cast.

I am unprepared. After the long close season and with no chance to practise I had expected it to take time to recover accuracy and length. But the line unfurls sweetly, the fly alights daintily, it floats towards him naturally and he takes it.

There is nothing skilled about my reaction. There is no measured pause and no controlled strike. Even as I see his nose and hear his sip I am snatching back the rod, losing my footing, losing my balance, shipping cold water. It shouldn't happen, of course. After all those years, with all that stored-up experience, it just shouldn't happen. But it has.

In the instant I am berating myself, in the split-second I have to recover some kind of composure, he jumps. It is a huge, furious, high-speed jump, but somehow the essentials imprint – the golden flank, the open jaw, the clicked fly, the splinters of light, the ebbing waves: gone. Just like that.

I did have my plans: the ones for reaching the rod high and hauling on the line and stepping calmly back, with everything designed to deprive him of freedom of manoeuvre; to keep him on top and deny him the dive. But they are as leaden and dead now as the weight I can feel.

The line runs from my rod to that terrible place behind the visible post, just as it did before. I have the same ache inside, anticipate the same scarring jag-jag; feel it. Everything goes slack.

I don't know how he did it, but he did. I don't know how I could have done it, but I have. All that winter dreaming, all that careful planning, all that will-he-or-won't-he and can-I-or-can't-I, all of it, all of it, over in a flash.

Someone turns up the colour and the sound. For some reason they are all still there: the water, the light, the meadows and the woods, the sky-high lark and the busying vole. The cuckoo, oh yes, the cuckoo.

What a sport this is. All of that tranquillity and then those tensions and dramas and now again this, just as before. It is, of course, all this, the whole amazing combination of it, that brings me back to the water year after year.

Wonderful: day one and maybe love-one, but a whole season to come.

A Rainbow Tries to Spawn

Rainbow trout were introduced to Britain over 100 years ago. They have been a boon to fishery owners and anglers alike. Compared with the brown trout they are cheap to produce and they fight much harder.

Rearing rainbows is now big business and – regrettably – many fish farms producing them have been sited on rivers. Escapes occur every year and then thousands of small fish – it is usually the small ones that escape – can take over whole reaches of water, driving native fish from their lies and sweeping up the available food. What in controlled numbers has been a benefit becomes, uncontrolled, a form of environmental pollution.

Mercifully, there are few waters in Britain where rainbow trout can spawn. Even if fish big enough to spawn manage to escape they cannot usually shed their eggs or milt, for reasons no-one fully understands. Of course, that does not stop them trying. FROM *The Times*, August 21, 1991.

Anyone who spends enough time in the countryside sees some remarkable things. Most of the remarkable things that anglers see, occur by the water.

I was walking slowly upstream, looking for the first rising trout.

It had been a glorious day. A blue haze quieted the valley. Cattle cogitated. Swifts sculpted the air. The first flies of evening were lifting into the sun.

I had just rounded the bend when I saw it; an odd movement, a heavy, spasmodic ebbing of rings close in by the distant bank. There were no sounds of duck, there was no sight of a vole. The water there was too shallow for a dabchick to dive in or swim. It was not the place for a trout to be: trout would be on the outside of such a bend where the water was deeper and where the current funnelled the flies into a thin, dense line; where it made them easiest to get with least energy expended.

I walked quietly on, looking hard.

The far bank was lined with rushes. Between the gravel bed midstream and the rushes, the river shallowed rapidly. A narrow, silted channel, perhaps a yard-and-a-half long, ran right through the rushes, into the bank.

Watercress grew on both sides of the channel, yellow flag iris flew tall at the end. As I drew opposite there came again, from right inside the channel that curious, spasmodic ebbing of ripples, that occasional, hesitant splash and, this time, the un-mistakable gleam from a big fish's belly.

When the commotion had stopped and the silt clouds had settled I saw a large trout lying on its side, head in towards the bank. Every two minutes or so it appeared to convulse, its tail arching repeatedly upwards, slapping and smacking back down on the water.

The movements were feeble but every flap of the tail inched the fish forward. The trout was clearly dying and every move-ment of its death throes was driving it forward into the bank. It was beaching itself head-first.

By the time I had found a place to wade over and had reached the spot, the fish was a pathetic sight, only just alive.

Its head was resting on a piece of cress below the water, its cheek lay a fraction under the surface. Of its entire body only the membrane of its rounded eye broke the surface, the yellow iris and black pupil exposed to the drying sun. It was a bizarre detail, one that magnetised my own eye, like something taken from a Hitchcock film.

The trout's body was covered in silt, not evenly but in a curiously barred pattern so that it looked quite like a perch.

There was silt in its gills. Its mouth lay open and, dreadfully, there was silt inside that as well.

I was wrestling with myself – to kill it outright or to leave it be – when the end came. There were a few more weak spasms. The fish's tail trembled and fretted. A pectoral fin lifted from its flank to leave a clean, bright space in the silt on the scales. The fin reached far out and twirled unnaturally. The lower jaw jerked sharply shut a half-dozen times, as though the fish were still trying to kill something hard and alive in its mouth.

Then the exposed eyeball tilted a little towards the nose, stared sightlessly at something finally arrived and rolled loosely back.

The dome of the sky looked down at it. Somewhere a blackbird sang. A trout sploshed in the current on the outside of the bend, where all trout should have been. Long moments passed before I made to stand up.

As I straightened, something again caught my eye; circular shapes, white or pink, lying on the silt.

There was no thinking time, but in the moment it took me to alter focus and look I was expecting to see petals, fallen from an overhead flower.

They were eggs. I counted 36 of them, 29 around the fish's body, seven others further back along the channel.

They were dead eggs, of course; white, some of them with just a touch of orange, all of them flaccid, half-full.

I looked back at the fish and touched her for the first time, then lifted her up. As she came to the vertical, her body hanging heavily, a thin rush of eggs poured down the trout's flank, streaming and plopping into the water. I had never seen such a thing on a river before.

I saw then that her vent was swollen and torn, that her fins were tattered and frayed. Her body, when I gently washed the silt away, was scratched from end to end. Her tail was half-eaten away.

With a tail like that, and in the state she was in, she had never been intended for the river. Somehow she had escaped from a fish farm further upstream; escaped from the hell of the holding pond where thousands of others like her will have been jam-packed, swimming in endless Orwellian circles, biting the tails of the fishes in front and being bitten, in turn, from behind.

Free in the wide waters and laden with eggs, she had sought out the kind of gravel in which she was programmed to spawn, the same gravel in which the wild trout of the river had themselves always spawned. And she had tried so hard to do what everything inside her urged.

She was not to know that the other fish were all brown trout. Nor was she to know that she was a rainbow or that her species had never become acclimatised here.

In over 100 years, rainbow trout have spawned successfully in only a handful of English streams.

She had no way of knowing that this was not one.

Three Deadly Dressings

The two sides have circled one another for years. The exact imitators have bobbed and weaved, the perfect presentationists have scored a quick point and backed away. It has seemed, this contest between imitation and presentation, an argument without end.

It has always puzzled me. Presentation has to be the vastly more important. No matter how perfectly a fly is made, it will not catch a fish that has been scared out of its wits by clumsy presentation. A poorly-dressed fly presented in an unalarming and natural way to a trout that is quietly feeding, may well cause the fish to take.

It is because I recognise that exact imitation – even if it could be achieved – is not necessary, that I no longer go to the lengths I once did, to imitate specific creatures in and on the water. The search for likeness is challenging and absorbing, but in practical fishing terms it is rarely necessary. At the water a simpler approach will do. FROM *The Times*, March 4, 1996.

I have, in my time, tried every kind of dry fly known to God and man and a few possibly not known to either. These days, though, I take the minimalist approach: I know that three simple dressings will meet most of my needs and it is on these that I concentrate.

This is not to deny the fascinations of fly tying or to suggest that other patterns are not sometimes useful. Mayflies will always be needed on mayfly waters when a hatch is on, daddy-long-legs come in handy for drawing up fish in lakes on hot summer days. Damsels can also prove useful for the same purpose or when a fish is obviously feeding on them.

Lakes, indeed, call for specific variation. On stillwaters, a couple of brighter flies based on the principle of 'calculated suggestion' (which I discuss at length in my book *The Pursuit of Stillwater Trout*) can be invaluable. In my experience, flies with bodies made of seal's fur or seal's fur substitute in distinctly visible but not startling colours – for example, some shades of off-red – are especially valuable.

These dressings do not have to look like specific flies, they simply have to look like food. The seal's fur traps air and, viewed from below, has a translucency which suggests – I recognise how subjective this is – 'goodness to eat'. In red or orange or some such it is also highly visible against the darkness of the mirror, which is where most flies are first seen by trout. And on lakes, where there is no current to take the fly to the fish and the fish must go in search of the fly, visibility can be of great importance.

Beyond these special-circumstance flies, all the dry flies I carry these days can be contained in a couple of those little plastic tubs that film comes in. One of them contains little brown jobs, the other contains little black jobs and, on rivers, I would feel well-armed with these alone.

For all the apparent handicaps of such an approach, consider, as always, the fish. It is lying some way below the surface, looking up. It recognises most flies by the tiny pinpoints of light where the insect's feet or body touch the surface. The fish knows how big these pinpoint patterns are: they are similar in size to the impressions made by every natural fly it has ever seen. These sizes – the occasional oddity excepted – are much of a muchness and can be imitated on hook sizes 18 to 12.

The fish also knows generally what colour natural flies are because the range is so limited. An unalarmed trout that is feeding at the surface does not agonise over every fly it takes. If it did, the hatch would be over and the fish would be one day nearer to death by starvation. If a feeding fish sees something of familiar size and colour and it has not been alarmed, there is a chance it will rise.

Many flies are black, from the minute and infuriating smuts to the black gnats. A plain black fly – black seal's fur body, black hackle – imitates these in all essentials in sizes 18 and 16. There is only one large black fly and that is the Hawthorn. The Hawthorn fly – it is a terrestrial insect that gets blown onto the water – appears from the middle of April to the middle of May. Then, the same dressing as above, on size 14 and even size 12, will do the job.

The other common flies which the trout take off the surface are the various olives and sedges. The typical colour of a newly-hatched olive is a drab grey-green or green-brown. The sedges, typically, are an overall brown.

I have not found trout feeding on hatching olives to be overly fussy about pattern – at least on rivers. The olives often hatch in vast numbers and trout feeding on them seem programmed to respond to light pattern alone. Nor, as a rule, have I found trout feeding on sedges to be overly concerned about patterns. And so I use a sedge pattern with a green-brown seal's fur body, short head hackle and wings of clipped hackle fibres laid along the back, to imitate both, in sizes according to the circumstance.

I use the sedge pattern even when olives are on the water because the fish seem untroubled by the difference and the sedge, having rather more body bulk than an olive dressing, floats longer.

There is an important point about the way these first two flies are fished. Mostly, I dunk my dry flies in flotant and then chuck them out so that they float high and dry on the top. There are times, however, when it is necessary to fish them not on the surface film, but in it. The fish often indicate these times by not taking. Then I grease only the top and back of the fly so that it settles well down into the surface before stopping. Takes to dry flies right on top can be splashy affairs. Takes to dry flies fished in the surface can be very confident – presumably because the fish takes as though eating a dead or dying fly or even an emerger which, through instinct, it knows cannot escape.

There is another, quite distinct dressing in my tub for little brown jobs. It imitates the olive spinners. Most olive spinners have sherry-brown bodies and clear wings that lie flat on the water, out to either side. Being clear, these wings allow light to pass through them from above, and so the brownish body of the fly and the pools of light transmitted by the wings are visible to the trout scanning the darkness of the mirror.

The light pattern the natural spinner makes is very different to the pattern created by my artificial sedge and so I carry a specific dressing to imitate it. The tails are conventional, the body is made from the same green-brown seal's fur mixture as the sedge, tied slimly, and the wings are made from a single, narrow slip of polythene cut from a kitchen bag. This slip is tied in the middle across the hookshank just behind the eye and it completes a dressing that is a dead-ringer for the natural insect. A tiny nick at the base of each wing will stop the fly spinning during the cast and kinking the leader.

This fly lies naturally flush in the surface film and the rise to it, as to the natural spinner, is a subliminal sip. It completes, when accurately cast, a deadly trio that will see many a season through.

Attention to Detail

There are some wonderful fly fishers about. Every trip to the water shows that. Not famous fishermen, not even fly fishers who write, just anglers who have mastered their art.

Such men have three qualities. The first is a knowledge of the fish in the water. The second, of course, is physical skill: the ability to approach the water in an unalarming way and to put their fly where they want it, fishing in the way they want it to fish. The third quality is less obvious and more general. It is a willingness to give attention to even the smallest detail. If a problem can be anticipated and solved, it is anticipated and solved. If tackle can be further refined, then it is further refined. Michael had all of these qualities. I once fished with him. FROM *The Times*, July 20, 1994.

I t is one of the joys of writing about fishing that readers so often react to what they see. Among the various brickbats and agreements, criticisms and compliments, suggestions for future pieces I might write and all else, there come invitations of various kinds.

Not uncommonly they include invitations to fish, or suggestions of places to fish – usually well-known waters to which the reader has access. Just occasionally invitations arrive to fish what one reader memorably called 'nameless places, mentionable only in whispers'.

I have just returned from a nameless place mentionable only in whispers – and then only to those who already know, in a sound-proofed room. It was that rarest of waters, an unpublicised English river with a reliable run of sea trout. The trip was especially memorable because I was able to witness the remarkable specialist skills of a quiet and modest angler.

The river that Michael invited me to fish was not on the sea trout map as most people know it. Yet at a time when the Irish sea trout are all but gone and many others, it seems, are going, this small, tucked-away river is providing sport with fish from 2lbs to 6lbs for a few tight-lipped locals.

There are, of course, some snags. One is that like sea trout everywhere, the fish do not give themselves up easily. Another is that, like sea trout in most shallow waters, the fish melt away during the day and so have to be fished for at night. These two hurdles alone mean limited success for most and limited interest from others. They also put the greatest fishing pressure on open reaches that lend themselves to casting in the dark.

Unlike many on the river, Michael catches fish pretty well every time out. He succeeds because he deserves to succeed and the place he took me to, the place he fishes most, showed why. It is the kind of place that few anglers would attempt to fish even if great trout had their heads above water and were demanding flies by the boxful.

The problem is the trees. The water runs through dense woodland. When we reconnoitred the stretch before dark, I could see that the river was as beautiful as I had been told. I could also see that it would be difficult to fish in that place during the day and virtually impossible by night.

Even wading in the middle of the river on a higher reach in daylight, fishing for the small brown trout with which the water is full, the trees had made the casting tricky enough. But where we were to fish at night there would be no question of wading because the water was deep and the bank was high. Then Michael showed me a half-dozen tiny spaces in the margins where an angler might fish. Of course, he would have to kneel down to do it. And of course, he would have to insinuate precise lengths of backcast through tiny gaps in the foliage that he would be unable to see. But still, Michael said, it was possible.

He pointed up and behind to the two or three snipped ends

of twigs that he had removed at each place to make an impossible cast through the canopy just achievable. He pointed to the two or three cut ends by each place at the waterside where a landing net could be reached down without snagging. The cuts were so few and so precisely located that in that jungle you would never have seen them, even if you had been looking.

When we returned to tackle up, Michael chose each of us a fly he had tied himself. Each individual fly was weighted a precise amount for each fishable spot under the conditions as we found them. We attached them to leaders that he had left soaking in washing-up liquid all day so that, from the first cast, they would cut cleanly through the surface film and avoid a wake.

When an early cast of mine reached behind and a tree side-stepped to grasp it, he offered me a tiny torch to help me sort things out. He had stuck a red plastic film over the glass so that the torch gave out only a soft, suffused glow. The light was good enough to work by, but not so strong that it would illuminate the canopy overhead in a way close-in fish might see, or silhouette us starkly when pointed away from the water.

When Michael fished his casting was, for all the reaching branches, precise and confident. Each movement of the rod was made with controlled vigour, the line hissing invisibly through the air, cutting into spaces in the foliage behind him that he could not see but knew were there.

We both settled down. The blackness grew deeper. Owls hooted, pheasants coughed, a distant fox barked. The Plough prickled through the clear patch of sky above the water where the trees on the banks did not quite meet. The mute grey ribbon of water slid smoothly in front of us, occasionally surging and rolling when a fish jumped or swam by.

We both touched fish, the soft pluck-plucking and the occasional, fearsome snatch from the blackness wrenching around the rod and making my heart pound and my blood roar. And then, as I was disentangling yet another snagged throw, Michael called softly from along the bank. He was 'in'.

I edged up the bank, feet feeling the way, arms outstretched. He was so low and still in the blackness that I almost fell over him. Crouched down, I felt and heard the deadly battle being fought: his wonderful confidence and control; the violent energy of the unseen fish; the only sound in that intensity of silence the occasional swirl at the surface and the soft zip-zipping from the rod-rings as the fish won line.

When the fish tired, the net was slipped through the known gap between the branches and the roots and then lifted back from the dark in a single, smooth movement. The first sea trout of his season, on the first outing of his season, was on the bank. It was a beautiful three-pounder. Then a chill mist arose and killed the fishing within minutes.

We packed up, talking softly of this and that, then picked our way back through the woods, started the car and pulled away to the town on the far horizon. The blackness folded in behind our lights.

The next morning, I had to move on. The next night, far away, I knew that Michael would soon be back on his river, on that place so secret it is mentionable only in whispers and then to known locals in a sound-proofed room.

It had been a privilege to fish such a water with such a man. There are some wonderful fly fishers about.

The Mayfly

Not all fly fishers have seen the mayfly, but those who have are unlikely to forget it. The mayfly, the true mayfly, is an unforgettable creature, big as a galleon. In the early years of this century many stories were told about the density of its hatches. Cars, even the slow old boneshakers of those days, had to be stopped when driven near some rivers and lakes so that their windscreens could be scraped clear of the mess. A train entering Kintbury station, in the Kennet valley, is improbably said to have skidded because there were so many on the line.

Alas, now all is not well with the mayfly. Some waters that once had it in plenty, now have few. Some waters that once had a few, now have none at all. Some day soon, our children may be taking their own children to see it if they can. FROM *The Times*, May 14, 1991.

The last two weeks in May bring one of the great remaining, gently declining, phenomena of the British countryside. They produce the most certain sport of the fly fisher's year; more big fish than the rest of the season taken together; always a clutch of tyros who will hit the headlines with a whopper.

The last two weeks in May bring 'Duffers' Fortnight'.

May brings the mayfly.

Everything about the mayfly is remarkable: its size, its beauty, the extraordinary punctuality of its annual appearances, the suffocating density of its hatches, the spectacular mating dances and then the flies' poignant, communal deaths: deaths on such a scale that they can turn whole reaches of river into a grey, sliding slurry of nymphal shucks, broken wings, twisting tails and arching, trembling bodies. Amid it all, the ebbing rings of gorging fish, oil out.

Ephemera danica is one of the Ephemeroptera, those beautiful and delicate flies which, as every angler knows, have long, slender bodies, long tails and finely-veined, translucent wings which they carry high over their heads like miniature chapel windows. The difference between the mayfly and its cousins is in size and distribution.

In the main, any two individuals of the other Ephemeroptera could comfortably stand side by side on the little fingernail. *Ephemera danica* does not look small even in the palm of the hand. The body is about an inch long, the wings stand a good inch tall and the three arching tails can reach two inches in length in the spinner.

Cold and heatwaves apart, the mayfly appears with astonishing predictability. Its first appearance on a given river or lake rarely varies by more than a day or two each year; and its disappearance about a fortnight later is similarly predictable.

On an 'early' water it will appear around the 15th or the 16th and disappear by the 30th; on a late water it will appear around the 27th or the 28th and be gone by about June 10th. Anglers book their holidays to coincide with it, some hoteliers profiteer on the strength of it.

It is not that the mayfly hatches in greater numbers than other flies, it is simply that it is so much more obvious. It takes up more space under leaves, where it hides away from the sun; it fills up more sky on the wing; flat on the water's surface, her eggs laid, her body spent and her wings outstretched and trapped in the film, the female looks enormous.

To be on the water when the mayfly are up and the trout are on them, is a memorable experience. The flies can flutter in the ears, catch in the hair, alight on the hand, hang from the rod. When the mating dance is on – when the stored-up hatches of several days take to the air, rising and falling along the bankside before mating and returning to the water whence they came – it can be a mistake to attempt to talk.

This is not the case on every river or lake, of course, or on every river or lake that supports the mayfly; but there are still a few of such strongholds left.

To be anywhere amid such a density of some insects could be disquieting or worse. Not so with the mayfly. *Ephemera danica* is so extraordinary and so beautiful, so symbolic of the freshness and promise of the new season, that it gives a headiness to the riverside that all creatures share. Swallows swat and swoop; finches scramble; coots dibble this way and ducklings dabble that. Spiders busy themselves darkly.

Striking images are everywhere. I can see again the trout that repeatedly leapt from the water to pluck mayflies from under an overhanging dock-leaf; the splinter of blue light as a kingfisher flashed by the end of my rod and took the one mayfly amid thousands that I happened to be watching; the controlled precision of a big fish beneath a willow that had switched from feeding on living flies to dead because it knew it could get them with less effort.

It is a sadness, then, that magnificent *Ephemera danica* is in decline. In spite of the vividness of some memories and the plenitude of the fly in some places, evidence mounts year by year that the mayfly is losing ground.

It has not been happening overnight, or consistently on the same front, or always in the same way; but happening it is, little by little.

In my own angling lifetime the mayfly has disappeared from parts of Wiltshire, Berkshire, Hertfordshire, Bedfordshire, Kent, Sussex, Dorset and even Hampshire itself, the cradle of dry fly fishing as a worldwide sport.

The assault upon it is many-angled and relentless, in the water and in the air.

Some causes are obvious and brutal – like over-abstraction which has simply sucked dry many of the small streams where mayfly once lived.

Other causes are more subtle and individually or collectively destroy the insect's habitat, over time. Land drainage schemes have caused rivers to rise and fall with unnatural speed.

Insecticides that end up in the water get less and less dilution. Fertilisers meant for the land are enriching the water, creating choking growths of algae which carpet the river and lake beds when they die.

Working the land to the water's edge and the shameful use by some trout farmers of rivers as sewers for their product's excreta, have changed not only water quality but the composition of the silts in which the mayfly nymphs burrow and grow.

There are subtler menaces, too. Even the removal of hedgerows has affected the mayfly in a subtle and deadly way.

Because the hatched mayfly can neither eat nor drink, she needs to avoid fluid loss while waiting to mate. That is one of the reasons she hangs from the undersides of leaves: it is cooler there and away from the direct rays of the sun.

But the loss of hedgerows and the gradual clearance of bank-side shrubbery have deprived the mayfly of many of her roosting places. Now feeble-flying *Ephemera danica*, unable to reach the shade she needs, increasingly is falling exhausted in the open meadows, which provide protection neither from the midday sun nor the midnight chill.

The result of it all is that there are fewer waters in which the mayfly can live; that fewer mayflies are leaving the water as year follows year; that fewer mayflies are regaining the water to mate and continue the species.

Not much of this will be apparent over the next couple of weeks. In most places the hatch will appear a little better or a little worse than that of last year or the year before. Most rods will still bend, trout will still jump and birds will still swoop on the water.

But in some places, inch by inch, the decline will be continued and perhaps become apparent and that will not merely be some local loss.

Duffers' Fortnight is ironically named. Sooner or later we will have to explain it to our children.

Trees and Trout

No fly fisher wants his fishing to be too easy because all interest and challenge would go. No fly fisher in his right mind wants his trout uncatchable because all point of the exercise would be lost. It is a question of balance. It is the same with every aspect of angling. It is true of fly casting.

Most of us, most of the time, do not want to agonise over where our backcasts have gone, because we want our principal concentration to be on the water in front. At other times some of us still want the odd tricky place available where we can creep and crawl because we enjoy the challenge of the throw. Yet how often it happens: how often we leave a well-loved hidey-hole one season, to return at the beginning of the next to find it tidied or destroyed. The long, dark months hold perils. FROM *The Times*, February 4, 1994.

This is a bad time of year for some fly fishers. It is the close season, the time when club members, keepers and owners are 'working on the river' and 'improving the fishing'.

Too often, both terms are synonymous with manicuring the banks and removing trees or shrubs and with sawing off overhanging branches. Too often, the aim is to make the fishing easier. A tree or shrub is felled to give access to a piece of water where exceptional trout lie. A branch is trimmed so that an angler's fly does not snag when he casts to the leviathan beneath it.

And that, too often, is as far as the thinking seems to go. It takes little account of the needs of fish or the reasons why exceptional trout might find a tree attractive. It takes little account of aesthetics. It takes little account of the need of many anglers to have their skills – such as they may be – sorely tested from time to time. Its practical effect is to take the natural edge off the fishing. Its logical conclusion is to reduce the skill level necessary to cast to each nook and cranny to that of the least skilled or determined.

The pattern is familiar. Overhanging trees, especially trees overhanging the outside of a bend with deep water beneath them, often attract or nurture big fish because they offer shade and a sense of security as well as food. Just as important, they provide protection from an angler's casts and keep his harassing figure at bay. They provide resting places where aquatic insects can alight until they are ready to mate and return to the water. They harbour caterpillars and beetles that sometimes fall in.

As a consequence, fish idling beneath trees usually live stress-free, food-filled lives. They are often confident enough to feed at the surface when trout elsewhere are burrowing into the weed, seeking protection from the light and the flailings up above.

Because these big fish are feeding at the surface, the ebbing ring that each rise makes can often be seen far away. Even if it cannot, the sippings and slurpings can be heard all about. And so the big fish beneath the tree or the branch becomes a known feature of the river: a target, but an unattainable target for many.

Frustration among the many sets in. Pressure mounts to have the tree or the branch removed so that this exceptional, surface-feeding fish may be cast to: or to have an obstructive branch with its glinting tracery of broken nylon and destroyed ambitions, cut back. One winter, it is.

Come the new season, wonderfully clean casts can be made to the spot where the great trout lived: but the fish cannot be caught because it has moved away. The tree or shrub or branch had been the reason for its presence in the first place. Removing the cover removes the attraction of the spot.

In due course, the great fish may be found in another, more accessible place, and caught with a cast more easily made. Someone will be satisfied. The man or woman who rejoiced in the challenges that the tree or branch presented, loses out.

Removing the obstruction also removes some of the attraction from the fishery. A tree is not only a keeper-in of shawled secrets, it is an aesthetic thing. Removing first one and then another and another as the seasons pass can and frequently does lead to banks that have about them an unnatural nakedness. This has happened on several pieces of water that I regularly fish and, indeed, characterises long reaches of major fly fishing rivers both north and south.

An awkward tree or branch left in place has other advantages. It encourages fieldcraft and wristy skills. It not only screens the fish from the angler but the angler from the fish. And it can offer atavistic delights. The creeping and crawling, the bobbing and weaving required to find a place from which an improbable cast might be made, provide some of fly fishing's deepest satisfactions. They carry 20th-century man back to the forest and glade: to an age when fishing was a means of survival, a form of hunting and not a sport.

Such interludes also, in the wide-eyed intensity and excitement of the stalk, legitimise a return by grown men to childhood: take them back to short-trousered days when tall grasses were places where Red Indians lurked and where trees screened animal dangers. Indeed, it is to this absorption, this legitimised return to earlier roots, that angling owes much of its appeal, for some.

Within the whole of angling, no specialisation is more constrained and absorbing than fly fishing. In almost all other branches of the sport, natural baits are used. These other branches of angling demand high skills, but they are skills designed to persuade fish to eat what they normally eat.

In fly fishing, natural baits are not used. The flies that we employ – the most interesting of them, anyway – are imitations of real insects and the name of the game is deception. In opting for the artificial fly made of fur and feather, restraint – the willing disavowal of some of the things that would make the fishing easier – is the fundamental premise.

And yet still too many see the first bankside essential as being to abandon restraint; to so clear and manicure and sculpt a water that there is no bolt-hole for the fish, no place that cannot be reached first time, by anyone.

This is not a plea for fly fishing to be made the preserve of masochists or Olympian performers, or for it to be reduced to a form of combat with an encroaching jungle. It is to say that in the management of waters where a range of skills needs to be given expression – and that means the vast majority of club waters – a sense of balance is needed and yet is too rarely achieved.

In winter, too often, the saw and the axe hold sway.

The Dry Fly on Stillwater

All manner of tactics and techniques have emerged from the big reservoirs – above all from those in the Midlands. The loch-style that so long held sway has been supplemented by effective means of fishing at every level from the lake bed to the underside of the surface film.

It is only of late that the surface film itself has received proper attention and that the dry fly has been examined anew. In the hands of some the dry fly on stillwater has emerged as a deadly weapon. First-class anglers are fishing it as much as they fish all subsurface techniques together and are achieving phenomenal results.

This is not chuck-it-out-and-wait dry fly fishing. It is thoughtful, sophisticated and much-practised dry fly fishing. Anyone coming to it for the first time, especially anyone with a limited opportunity to practise, needs to devise for himself a clear plan of attack. I certainly devised one of my own. Here it is. It has since delivered some excellent results. FROM *Salmon and Trout*, Spring 1994.

Until a few years ago, if a man used the dry fly for five per cent of his fishing time on lakes, he was using it more than most. Now the technique is the preferred approach for many experienced reservoir men, in a wide range of conditions.

Of late I have fished the reservoirs less often than I used: I just have rivers nearby and so I have fished these when I could. In the last couple of years, though, I have fished Chew, Blagdon and Bewl with acknowledged experts in fishing the dry fly from a boat. I used the technique alongside them, for interest. There was no sense of competition, but their results were significantly better than mine on each occasion. This was not coincidence: they were just better than me. Their returns reflected a difference in skill, born of familiarity and experience with the technique.

They were days that set me thinking. I cannot get to the big lakes regularly and so will not have the opportunity to give serious attention to dry fly fishing, at least in the short term. However, I know that many anglers do fish the dry fly on reservoirs regularly and fail. They read the books and articles – and still they blank or struggle.

What we all need when tackling something new is a sense of purpose, a compass for moving from here to there. I thought it might be helpful to those who are facing the same challenges that I face to make some suggestions in this regard. They are based on the kind of thoughts that will guide my own dry fly fishing on lakes from now on, even though it will take some time for the results to come through. The aim is to suggest definite courses of action for those who would like to have them: hopefully to give a coherence and sense of purpose to what can, in the short term, so easily demoralise.

The thoughts are based on some assumptions. The first is that in seeking their experience most folk do not have dry-fly experts in the boat with them, to help. The second is that if they had, the expert would be taking fish when they were not: in other words, there are definitely fish around the boat and certainly more are willing to take than the struggler's results might suggest. To add realism, no fish are rising (and so, for example, simple accuracy in covering a sighted rise is not the issue – helpful though that ability always is). The final assumption is that a team of three or four flies is being used because the results of the experts and my own experience to date suggest that this is an advantage.

Given these assumptions, three possible reasons for not catching fish suggest themselves. The first is that the fish simply cannot see the flies on offer. The second is that the fish can see the flies full well, but do not like what they see: in other words, either the fly dressings, or the manner of presentation, or both, are wrong. The third possibility is that the fish can see the flies, may well like them and perhaps even are taking them – but that the offers are going unnoticed. All three possibilities need to be addressed.

To counter the possibility that the fish are not seeing the flies, the need is to manipulate in a sensible way those factors that can increase visibility – notably colour and size. Experiments should also be conducted with movement – but more of that, later.

When choosing dry flies, I would suggest dressings that are the sizes and colours of natural insects on the point and in the middle, but would experiment constantly with the sizes and colours of the flies on the top dropper. My aim would be to seek for dry fly fishing – a technique in which the flies are usually left immobile – something to replicate the powers of fish attraction that a bob fly dribbled over the surface gives to the wet fly practitioner.

I would expect the attractor fly to be taken some of the time; but I would expect most takes to come to the more natural dress-ings as fish, having been drawn up to investigate the attractor, notice them when turning away.

On the matter of presentation – individual fly patterns, leader length and diameter and so on – I would recommend those presentation factors that I use myself.

The point and middle flies should be in sizes 16 to 10, though the attractor would in the cause of experimentation be any size. The two 'natural' flies would in the first instance be chosen from the three I have discussed elsewhere (see Three Deadly Dressings, page 17) or any other dressing in which the angler has faith. They would be supplemented by the off-red and similar patterns I suggest in the same section for the reasons outlined there and by a couple of hatching nymphs.

The dry flies would sometimes be covered in flotant, so that they ride on top and sometimes greased along the back only so that they settle well down into the film, suggesting dead or trapped insects. Even flies of the same kind should be treated in these different ways and fished simultaneously, to see if reaction to the two varies.

For the leader I would use nylon fine enough to enable small flies to be fished naturally and of a diameter which literally thousands of trout have shown me they can accept at the surface in other circumstances: that is, 4lbs standard nylon or 6lbs double-strength. (Double-strength or pre-stretched nylon is brittle and a soft-actioned rod in the AFTM 5–7 class is the ideal weapon.) I would opt for an overall leader length of 15ft to 20ft or so, depending on the wind and the size and weight of the point fly, all of which influence leader behaviour in the air.

The third possible reason why some boat anglers struggle while experts take fish consistently in similar conditions, is that the experts are seeing and then capitalising on every take they get, whereas the average man is not. I believe this to be a much more important point than most anglers realise. Certainly I think it has been a likely factor in my own modest performance with the dry, so far.

There are many distractions while adrift with a companion. The lift and slide of the boat, the constantly-changing light and shade in the ripple, the soft and absorbing conversations, the day-dreaming, the general mental spilling-free that this lovely kind of day can offer all conspire, I am sure, to make me fail to see at least some delicate sips-in and rejections. I would see and respond to such offers when river fishing, or when lake fishing alone from the bank: but in the boat, for all the reasons above, I am sure I fish less intensely than I sometimes might – and so some offers go undetected.

Certainly, some experiences suggest this to be so. I have several times turned over fish when lifting off, that took me by surprise. There has to be a very good chance that these fish already had the fly in their mouths, which would be clear evidence that I had not seen them take it from the surface. This argues for knowing precisely where each fly is, all of the time, and for much greater concentration than usual.

The only other possibility about those fish surprisingly hooked is that they were near the fly at the moment I happened to lift off and the movement induced them to grab instinctively. This leads to another suggestion. It is that we all might try to replicate the possible stimulation of the lift-off by moving our flies a sudden foot from time to time, preparing ourselves for a sudden, answering snatch.

I would go further and suggest that the flies are recast frequently, as a matter of routine. This device would shift the balance from passive attraction, as it were, to active: the angler will be spending less time hoping fish will find his flies and more time seeking fish – perhaps provoking instinctive takes from fish newly in the area, reacting to the sudden arrival of food from above.

Naturally common sense has a role: the flies have to be given a chance to fish and the water cannot usefully be lashed into foam. But still I recommend repositioning the flies quite often.

And that is about it. The thoughts above form, I believe, the beginnings of an approach to a problem many anglers who recognise the value of the dry fly on stillwaters, are facing. They are based on nothing more than limited experience and a little common sense, but there are many worse starting places for any plan of action. They set out the principles that will be guiding all my own dry fly experiments on stillwater, from now on.

Falling in

Fishing has changed much over the years. Even in my own time there have been all manner of changes: changes in technology and tactics and technique; changes in river management and stocking patterns and the rest.

There have been other, more subtle developments; developments which are altering our enjoyment by the water. Some genuine small delights are being lost, possibly for good. I have in mind the little pleasures that old hands used to be able to take when disaster befell the innocent or the awkward: in particular when newcomers immersed themselves in their fishing more literally than they might have planned. It is a loss to be lamented and set on the record. Future generations should know what they have missed.

Falling in is not the thing it was. Once upon a time you could rely on seeing someone, somewhere, get a soaking most seasons. These days, people do not seem to have their hearts in it. Duckings are comparatively rare. Either anglers today are less adventurous than of old; or the banks and riverbed are being smoothed and manicured to the point of artificiality in the name of 'improvement'; or else when someone does take a ducking, the faller or duckee is wearing one of those namby-pamby, toe-to-neck neoprene body-waders that would keep him dry were he to be held under Niagara.

And where is the pleasure in watching someone fall in when he is wearing a garment that will keep him dry and comfortable? There is no pleasure at all.

It is because fallings-in, honest-to-goodness, thoroughly miserable soakings seem in danger of extinction that I have decided to set out, for the sake of the record, some of the principal varieties that the regular angler in my youth might have witnessed.

The Bellyflop was the most common. The Bellyflop is usually executed from a high bank with quite deep water cutting beneath it. There may well be trees about and a few shrubs and brambles. The essential is the hidden root; or the wire that runs at ankle height between two fallen posts; or perhaps the rabbit hole.

In the Bellyflop the progression is always the same. The foot catches, the arms are thrown rigidly high overhead – ideally grabbing for some saving branch which, of course, is not there. The hands open. The fingers splay out. The rod falls. A look of horror or terror is hopefully glimpsed, with the eyes bright and wide and the mouth open. Then comes the downward, cruciform free-fall of five, six and seven or more feet.

The Bellyflop is a dramatic fall – I know to some tastes almost melodramatic – but it can be deeply aesthetic if viewed from a low, dry bank. If the light is behind the faller, the upward showering of spray can take on the aspect of flung diamonds.

The Trip-and-Tumble or 'Forward Roll' as it is sometimes known, is executed in similar circumstances to those of the Bellyflop, though the progress and entry are quite different.

As before, the bank is high. There is the root, the wire, the rabbit hole. But in the Trip-and-Tumble the duckee has a little longer to be aware of his predicament. There is the same suddenness, the same initial, unstoppable forward momentum as in the Bellyflop, but this time the rod does not fall free. This time the rod – ideally it is an old and treasured rod, or else one of great value – catches in the grass and takes on a surreal curve not unlike that of the sickle moon at harvest time, but sharper towards the tip.

The angler sees the curve beginning, brings his empty hand down in a desperate and, of course, vain attempt to free the rod and the body begins a bending motion which cannot be halted.

The rod fractures with a slow, fibrous splintering; there is a strangled, half-articulated cry and entry is achieved immediately afterwards in a curled or semi-rolled position.

The Trip-and-Tumble does not have the free-falling, almost sky-diving abandon of the Bellyflop; and it does not, because of its rounder, cleaner entry, produce the same great splash and eddying of waves. It is an altogether more compact fall. Many connoisseurs, however, feel that what is lost in water and form is more than made up for by the clear sound of the rod snapping at the moment of maximum stress for the duckee.

As ever in angling, there are those who brag of having seen bigger and better; or who claim that the ultimate Trip-and-Tumble was the reported fall sighted somewhere in North Yorkshire in 1991, when entry was said to have been achieved in full foetal position following the fracture of seven rods, two of them split-cane.

However, I have never accepted this alleged fall and nor have others whose opinions I trust. I have yet to witness a full-foetal entry and no-one I know has found a first-hand witness to the alleged Yorkshire incident. I continue to regard the five-rod fall of Major Arnold Blinkthrice into the River Windrush in 1977, as the greatest, fully-authenticated Trip-and-Tumble. The weather that day was appallingly cold and Major Blinkthrice had to face a long walk back to his car in a biting wind. What is more, all the rods he broke belonged to his father-in-law, were rare and expensive and – the clincher for me – were without a penny of insurance cover.

The Backward Stagger is, of course, a classic. The angler is on the high bank and a companion calls; or a large bird breaks suddenly from a branch close to his head; or, if he has inadvertently walked past three 'Private Fishing' signs and crawled under a barbed-wire fence or two without noticing, a bailiff looms up unexpectedly. The angler, who already has a forward momentum, half-turns and catches his foot on our trusty root or in the ever-reliable rabbit hole.

He reels. He staggers backwards at an angle of 30 degrees to the vertical (or even the horizontal). His arms whirl entertainingly backwards, windmillesque. His feet back-pedal furiously in an attempt to resume their position beneath the head and shoulders. Then that wonderful entry begins, that stern-first pitch into the void with the beginnings of a part-somersault, always with an accompanying cry.

There are two other duckings that can occur from a bank – 'fallings-in' is not the right term in these cases – that I will mention for the sake of completeness, even though I do not rate the entries themselves very highly.

The Slide, the protracted, irresistible slippage down a shingled bank into deep water, is self-explanatory. The Strategic Retreat needs description.

The Strategic Retreat takes place from the bankside, often where a piece of open meadow abuts the river. There may well be signposts about the place, but too far away to be read or else turned the other way.

The Strategic Retreat is usually preceded by the sound of thundering hooves, or by a snort (followed by the sound of thundering hooves). Or by the sighting of a cloven hoof raking the ground. Or by the sudden glimpsing of a lowered head, with the space between two rather attention-getting horns covered in interesting, tight little curls. Or, in another circumstance entirely, by the sudden appearance of two large bailiffs when the presence of even one medium-sized bailiff might be deemed unhelpful.

The Strategic Retreat – you may already have guessed it – involves no more than a deliberate running and jumping into the water to escape. The duckee is soaked, it is true. Farmers may guffaw, beginners may be amused, some men of the cloth might laugh when later alone. But the Strategic Retreat lacks the involuntary suddenness of entry of the great Falls and Tumbles and must lose marks because of that.

Immersions that occur while the duckee is wading are in the main less fulfilling for the observer than those which occur from the bank. Even so, there are two honest-to-goodness soakings which can occasionally be seen if the right piece of riverbed can be found and camped by long enough; or if a particularly clumsy wader can be persuaded into the water where the bottom is uneven and the currents are likewise.

The first is the Slow Subsidence. This is the one in which the angler is wading in a rocky stream. The riverbed is covered with stones and shingle which the winter floods have thoughtfully rearranged.

Searching feet touch and grope and feel their way forward. Sometimes awkward rocks are encountered and circumnavigated. Then a seemingly solid purchase is found on a patch of gravel that might be recognised from a previous year and the weight of both feet is entrusted to it. But this year, the duckee discovers, the gravel and shale is not as extensive as it was, or not the shape that it was and naturally any wading stick has been left on the bank.

The false move is made, the slip downward begins. The water – and this being a rocky, upland stream the very cold water – reaches the top of the waders and spills down inside. The slider continues to sink, the water reaches those parts that would recoil if they could but cannot and an outburst of breath not unlike 'A-A-R-R-G-H' escapes the wader's lips. With a smooth and sometimes quickening motion, the duckee goes right in, the water sublimely welling up around his waist, his chest and perhaps briefly, his head.

The Drift-and-Bob likewise is not falling in according to the strict meaning of the term, but it can result in treasured memories. It will be familiar to old hands who have used chest-waders – those baggy, rubber chest-waders that are like thigh-waders with tops – on upland rivers.

The riverbed, this time, is stable and gently sloping. It is covered with small rounded stones with here and there a larger one. The current is swift and the desired fish – one or more, it matters little – are a little beyond casting distance, downstream and across.

For the Drift-and-Bobber, cast after cast falls short and cast after cast ends with the feet edging forward. The eager angler tries ever harder and concentrates ever more intently; and in his concentration and effort becomes ever-more buoyant without noticing. Only when it is too late – and ideally when an exceptional fish has been hooked – does the once firmly-rooted angler realise that he is tripping downstream on tip-toe, ballerina-style; that he has become a plaything of the eddies and currents; that the pool is much longer than he had realised, and deepening.

The sight of such an angler fully seized with the inevitability of it all, being buoyed downstream by the air in his waders while his legs scrabble wildly and feel nothing and his fish – potentially, perhaps, a record fish – heads upstream and around the bend, is a moment to be treasured.

There are other falls, of course, that are possible from points other than the bankside or the streambed, which can give a degree of pleasure when viewed from secure, dry land.

Most of these are what as boys we called Jetty Jobs – most commonly the Vertical Plunge (through loose or ancient planks) and The Splits (where the duckee attempts to step into a boat that he believed to be securely tied up). But beyond that, one is scratching.

I am often asked which is my own favourite fall. In these bank-manicured, neoprene-suited, namby-pamby days one cannot afford to have favourites. One has to settle for what one can get. Every one of the falls I have described is a delight to watch, imprinting itself on the memory split-moment by split-moment, to be enjoyed season and season through.

I have loved them all.

The Reel-smoker

I am not sure why a trout hooked in shallow water should run further and faster than a fish hooked in the deeps, but every fly fisher knows this is generally the case. Maybe it is because in shallow water the fish has only one place to go whereas in, say, the middle of Grafham or Rutland, it has two. Maybe it is because in addition to the alarm of being hooked a fish feels more exposed with the sun on his back and is instinctively trying to find sanctuary in some distant, known gloom. Either way, a good trout in the shallows will run long and hard. He can be a formidable opponent.

Then there is the bonefish. The bonefish is a creature of the tropical and sub-tropical flats, vast areas of knee-deep, thought-clear water that reach out from land under a baking sun.

No fish that I have ever heard of or angled for runs as far, as often, as the bonefish. At home, with trout, even where they run big, we see our backing only from time to time. On the light-winking flats of the Caribbean and the central Pacific, every bonefish of 3lbs upwards will take us deep into the backing, several times. I cannot imagine how they do it – what dynamic forces are at work, where they can find that energy. Yet they do. The bonefish is a seering fish, the father and mother of the reel-smoking run. It is a thrilling fish to see and stalk. Here is the story of my first. FROM *The Sunday Times*, September 11, 1988.

It was as though the world had stopped.

For 20 minutes the 18-ft skiff had thundered and planed

across the melted-crystal shallows off the middle Florida Keys. At 50mph, driven by the 120 horse-power outboard, the boat had ducked and draked the slow surface swell with wind buffeting my cheeks, hair flailing my ears, the mud and coral seabed flashing by an uneasiness beneath our backsides like high-speed film, now light green, now dark; now brown and grey; now red and indigo and blue.

Only moments before we had been banking like an aircraft around islands and sandbars; had taken a line of ancient marker-posts like a slalom; had left the water completely, twice.

And then we shut off the engine. The skiff physically sank, the water hushed against the bows and Ed Cale, my professional guide, a man with the eyesight of a stooping hawk, reached for the long pole he would use to punt us through the fishing grounds, and perched on the high platform that bridged the engine.

We were fishing at last.

Close by, the long, bare roots of mangrove trees stapled a dozen small islands to the seabed. A frigate bird on outstretched, sheath-knife wings, chinked and jousted with a thermal, toying with the air, playing with it in a way that bordered on the self-indulgent. The soft moccasin of the tropical morning – 89 degrees Fahrenheit, 82 per cent humidity – pressed down.

Ed saw it first.

'There's a mud.' A mud is the term the guides use for the silt fish often disturb when they move onto the shallows to feed.

'It's bonefish all right. I saw the disturbance a long time ago and thought it might be a ray. But it's definitely bonefish. I saw their tails.'

I followed his arm and finger pointing downwind and then, eventually, I saw it too: the small, elongated milky stain in the water, slowly lengthening almost 200 yards away.

'You make ready, I'll head them off' and then, with a long, steady push on his pole he began to ease us across and down-wind.

My limbs weren't working very well. I'd made the 10-hour flight from London for this moment above all and now, when it had come, every muscle and joint trembled with an electric charge that had nowhere to go. My fingers thickened as I unhitched the fly from the rod-ring. When I stripped line onto the deck in making ready to cast, it tangled around the reel, caught under my feet. The boat seemed suddenly less steady, from my knees down.

I'd read a lot about bonefish. Many of my friends had told me about them: animated torpedoes encased in beaten steel; fish so fast and powerful they had caused fly-reels to seize, lines to jam, strong hooks to open; fish so wary and highly strung when they come onto the shallows in daylight, that they could be put to flight by an exhaled breath.

I exhaled no breath that I can recall, from the beginning of the encounter to the end. We moved towards the cloud of silt, Ed preoccupied with his pole. The silt moved towards us, the bone-fish, somewhere near its upwind edge, preoccupied with their feeding: with their rummaging and rooting on the bottom for small crabs and shrimps, now and then one of them standing on its nose to take something from the bottom, its tail, like some great, soft scythe, slicing the water's surface, working this way and that. And I was preoccupied with my tensions, making ready.

Forty yards upwind of the 'mud', Ed stopped, his pole holding the bottom just inches below our keel, the only sound the soft, hollow, pat and lap of water against the skiff's sides. The air tingled.

Thirty-five yards. Thirty. Twenty-five yards. At twenty-five yards I saw the fish themselves for the first time: half a dozen of them; shadows materialising and melting, resolving and dissolving beneath the sun-pricked, winking surface. Ed and I both crouched low.

At 20 yards, I cast. Not far enough. I cast again instantly, let the fly settle for a few moments, and then gave it the merest, life-suggesting tweak. A shade detached itself slightly from the group and a tail broke the surface where I knew my fly to be. As the tail went down and I knew the fish had levelled off again, I tightened.

In an instant, before I could gather my once well-ordered wits, the rod was wrenched down and the fish launched itself on a relentless, unstoppable run, the bow-wave it made spreading a rapidly-widening V across the thin water to our right. The fish was 100 yards away and more before it paused, and then it had another 30 yards of line around a mangrove stump before I realised that all the while, Ed had been poling after it, trying to keep pace.

Lifetimes later – Ed reckoned 10 minutes – I got the fish to the boat, unhooked and photographed it, and then slid it back into the water. It lay still for a few moments, its gills slowly opening and closing. And then it began to move away, dematerialising in a matter of yards when we could see every strand of weed around it, every discarded shell, for miles.

It was an ethereal climax to an ambition achieved. I was a truly happy man.

And then somebody started up the world again. A brown pelican on huge, drooping, hang-glider wings, slid noiselessly overhead. A flying fish played ducks and drakes with itself. In the blue middle limbo of steamy, early morning, a far-away speedboat hummed like a sewing-machine and stitched a white thread through the wavelets. Ed lit a cigarette. I opened a Coke.

It hadn't been a big bonefish. At 7lbs or so it had been an average bonefish for the Keys and later in the day we were to see (though not catch) many far bigger. Yet the whole, hair-triggered experience of fishing for it alone, and catching it alone, had been worth the 9,000-mile return flight, the lost sleep, the hassle about the car, the electrical storms and the 20-odd inches of rain that in the last few days had come down in rivets, mostly on me.

Almost always (and naturally) when at home and we think of fly fishing, we think in terms of freshwater: saltwater fly fishing is unknown in Europe in any comparable sense. In Florida, parts of the Gulf of Mexico and much of the Caribbean, saltwater fly fishing is a well-developed and thrilling sport – and the essential skills needed are those that are used by trout fishermen every day. It is only the scale of things that differs: the area of stalkable water (for all practical purposes, it is limitless); the extreme wariness of the fish; and above all their size and power.

Many fish are stalked with the fly in Florida. The biggest of them all and, after the bonefish the one I most wanted to catch, is the tarpon: it grows to eight feet long, can weigh 300lbs and often it feeds near the top.

The sight of such a magnificent creature slicing through the water's surface towards you for all the world like a gigantic, smutting trout, knowing that it is a potential taker of the fly you have deliberately laid in its path, and have remained attached to of your own free will, is almost paralysing.

I had just one opportunity to try for a tarpon and astonishingly I made contact at once.

It was, of course, the skill of my guide Jimmy Fox that put me in the fish's path. He did it with a precision Hiawatha would have admired, a mile or so off Indian Key.

I had just joked about the weight of the fly-rod Jimmy had given me to use – 'it's a bit like a billiard cue, but not as whippy' – when the first fish showed and my voice drained away.

It was the leading fish in a group of three or four and as they came towards us, rolling and sheering through the surface, I could hear the water sluicing and peeling off their vast, brown backs and metalled, iridescent silver sides. The fly-rod, suddenly, seemed a pathetic thing.

With some effort – such a rod leaves little room for wristy finesse – I dropped the four-inch lure ahead of the nearest fish, paused and then moved it a yard. I felt the whole line lock solid, saw a tarpon of around 120lbs lollop idly through the surface and then continue on its way. The next moment my rod-arm was educated to the horizontal, the stretching line sang a high brief tune as I tried to set the hook and then it came back to me, my fly gone at a knot.

I had not troubled that fish in any way: it simply had not known that I was there.

There is, of course, the other angling experience available in Florida: the classic experience made famous by Hemingway, Zane Gray and the others: big-game, deep-sea fishing for marlin and sailfish.

Hemingway, in one angling piece, reported such an

abundance of marlin in the 90-mile strait between Key West and Havana that in one afternoon, while playing one marlin, six others passed close to the boat in half an hour.

Things are not like that any more. Leastwise, they're not off the Keys. Captain Larry Dukehart, who took me out from Islamorada to try, reckons it takes 14 days' fishing to get attached to a marlin, now. Experienced big-game men I've spoken to say they would regard that as optimistic, for Florida.

The reason, of course, is over-exploitation. The Floridians have been more profligate with their big-game resources than most – and that's saying something. Now, all the fishermen of the Keys have got conservation, Ayatollah-style. Absolutely everything that's not going to be eaten for food – and strict (and small) bag limits prevail – goes back, or else. The days of the chest-beating parades on the quays, are over.

With self-discipline, of course, the good times might return. But they will take years a-coming. In the meantime, the big-game men still congregate and still they pursue great fish. Moby Dick is alive and well and out there somewhere, for those who are hooked on the hunt and the surge of their own adrenaline.

Big-game fishing is fantasy stuff, an experience I would not have missed even though it is a light-year away from my beloved trout.

The Man o' War, like all these big-game boats, is medallion-man with muscles. Its great outriggers, controlling huge lures far behind the boat, droop under their own weight and the pressure of the slipstream; rods that could lift a mule are ranked at the ready, their great, heavy-metal multiplier reels upturned to the sun. Fighting chairs are bolted to the deck, harnesses lie in lockers, ready to buckle on and take the strain if a big fish strikes.

When the fleet puts out at dawn, the boats look like great white chariots drawn by stallions, the dark squares of the cockpit windows, the clean verticals of the bows sustaining the image: charging knights with their visors down.

Larry Dukehart's skill caught me a lot of fish from the indigo waters of the Gulf Stream, the biggest a 70-lb amberjack that I winched up 250ft at the height of a tropical downpour. But

Moby Dick swam safe and free, just as he had during the rest of my stay.

One reason, of course, was that I'd had so little time on the water: I'd lost four full days in the seven to unseasonably long storms (which was nobody's fault); and another was that I'd been let go by the tarpon (which was probably mine).

Transcending all, however, is the fact that I got my bonefish and had the wind not suddenly sprung up, I might have had several more. The world really did stop that morning by the mangrove trees and I have one professional guide, and one photograph of a truly happy man, to prove it.

Hugh Falkus

Many men have made contributions to angling. Some men have made great contributions. We know what these contributions are because mostly they have come to us in the form of books and we have the books to read.

By and large we know little about the men to whom we owe these debts – about the work they did, the kinds of people they were, the life experiences that forged and drove them. There must have been many fascinating individuals among these authors but the details that would have illuminated them are lost.

Few who have had any connection with angling can have led a fuller or more fascinating life than Hugh Falkus. With his death on March 30th, 1996, twentieth-century angling lost one of its great figures. The world also lost a man of extraordinary energy, intellect, creativity, physical courage and sporting prowess.

The contribution made by Falkus will live through his books and, to a lesser extent, through his films. However, the details of his extraordinary life, unless captured and set down could well, like those of other pioneering figures, be lost with time. We are too cavalier about our great men. Many, I know, feel this way. That is why these notes, most of them not associated with angling at all, are included here.

I knew Hugh Falkus, on and off, for the last 20 years of his extraordinary life. We first met – I cannot quite remember the circumstances – in a bar in the West End of London. A number of things have stuck about the meeting. The first was his physical appearance: he was tall, powerfully-built, blond and handsome. There was the fact that in that carpeted and pinstriped place he wore a thick country suit in olive green and made everyone else look awkward. There was the fact that we got on so extraordinarily well: that we agreed on almost everything fishy we discussed, from angling technicalities to angling issues. Over the following years we exchanged inscribed books, corresponded, rang one another from time to time, occasionally held a rendezvous, always in London.

We last met on the afternoon of October 29th, 1995. I had gone to see him because I knew he was ill. It was a bright, crisp day. A misty start had given way to blue skies and feathers of thin, high cloud. The leaves on the oaks and chestnuts were rusting. Red berries warmed the hedgerows on the winding Cumbrian roads. The low fells all around were lit with a slanting, gold-leaf light. The River Esk, below the cottage where Hugh and his wife Kathleen lived was low and clear. Here and there a salmon lay.

Hugh had lived in Cragg Cottage since his marriage. Kathleen had lived in it or beside it all her life, was the local farmer's daughter and had been born on the land. It would be difficult to imagine two more differently-lived lives, so intimately juxtaposed. After three previous marriages on Hugh's side, Kathleen and he were together for 38 years.

Hugh was late down. He normally got up at around midday but that morning had been up at seven. A friend had died some days before and, with a group of others, Hugh had been to the river to scatter the ashes on a favourite pool. Champagne had flowed, as it sometimes does on these occasions. Hugh had gone back to bed on his return and had fallen soundly asleep. When he came downstairs at 2.30pm instead of noon he still had his pyjamas on under his clothes. He was full of apologies. I always found him the most courteous of men.

We went first to the fishing hut owned by his great friend and neighbour Bill Arnold, a man who had done Hugh innumerable kindnesses in later years and with whom he had collaborated on several sporting projects. We talked for a while under the great, glass-cased sea trout on the wall, surrounded by photographs of angling triumphs and beaming faces, some familiar. Then the light began to fade and the autumn chill began to creep in. We drove the few hundred yards back to 'Cragg', settled ourselves in his warm study and talked on for several hours more. Finally, declining the offer of dinner and a bed and with the prospect of my own long drive to come, I said farewell.

That day's conversation, together with earlier conversations remembered and much rummaging among yellowed cuttings in the library of *The Times* and elsewhere, forms the basis of the detail in the notes which follow.

Hugh Falkus – Hugh Edward Lance Falkus – was born in Cheam, Surrey, on May 15, 1917. His father, who had worked in the City, retired first to the Essex marshes and then to Devon, where the family lived on a boat moored in various estuaries. It was in these two wide land and seascapes that Hugh spent his youth, when not away at school or being kept at a desk by some tutor at home. He lived the life of a free spirit in those early years, mostly with a rod or a gun in his hand, or a keel beneath his seat. His father seems to have been forever alongside, though never his mother – about whom Hugh was always reluctant to speak. Hugh caught his first fish when he was four, learned to shoot when he was six and was a successful competitive helmsman by the time he reached his teens.

By 18 he had learned to fly and by 20 he was in the Royal Air Force, headstrong and brilliant. He had many brushes with death, not least because of his penchant for aerobatics, regardless of the aircraft he was flying. He once memorably – and very nearly fatally – looped a lumbering Handley Page bomber, taking it up to 17,000 feet and only levelling out a little above the ground.

His most amazing escape came in more serious circumstances, not long after he had married Doris Walters, a childhood sweetheart. In 1941, by now a Spitfire pilot, he was scrambled to intercept enemy bombers. Hugh shot down two and became so intent on finishing off a third he had already hit, that he was himself brought down over France. He fell into German hands wearing only pyjamas under his flying suit. The SS interrogated him, concluded that because of his unconventional dress he must be a spy, beat him up and decided to execute him.

Hugh was taken out and a firing squad was facing him. As a last act of defiance he turned his back on the raised rifles. There was a stream running close by and he saw a trout rise in it. Hugh decided that in what he fully expected to be his final moments, he would concentrate all attention on that fish. Before the order to fire could be given a German staff car swept up, a Wehrmacht major-general got out, barked a few questions and then bundled Hugh into the rear seat and drove away. It turned out that he had been educated in England. That night Hugh drank champagne through broken teeth before military formality reasserted itself and he was taken away to a prison camp.

Four grim years followed in camps in France, Poland, Germany and Silesia – so grim that when, in the mid-1980s a mutual friend gave me a photograph of Hugh posing with other prisoners of war and I sent it to Hugh for interest, he returned it at once with simply two words – 'Horrible Place' – scribbled on a piece of notepaper.

Hugh made numerous attempts to escape. He worked on 13 tunnels, including the famous Wooden Horse tunnel, finally breaking out and getting back to England only days before the war ended. It was not long afterwards that his first marriage failed.

Hugh told me that on his return, 'I decided that no-one was going to give me another order. No-one was going to shout at me again. I am going to be on my own...whatever it is. I am going to be myself.' As the Germans had found out while they had him and many others who had encounters with him were subsequently to discover, Hugh had the intellect, will and force of personality to ensure that he was never beaten down. He said what he meant and meant what he said. For the rest of his working life, Hugh freelanced.

At first he went on the stage using skills he had learned in the prison camps, mostly as a director and actor. 'I loved every minute of it, found I had a talent for it. I did everything except sing and dance.' Then he began to get work from the BBC. By 1949 he was presenting live television from Alexandra Palace, writing and narrating for radio – and fishing, shooting and sailing whenever he could.

His fishing even at this time proved to have a future significance. He had already discovered the Cumbrian Esk and often fished it with an ex-RAF friend who lived near the river. He would write and read a morning story at Broadcasting House in London, be handed his cheque – 'in a brown envelope, on a silver salver' – dash across London in a taxi and take the train north. He would fish all night, fall exhausted into the first train south and sleep on the journey. Back in London at 3pm, he would take a taxi straight to the BBC again to work on that evening's *Children's Hour*. It was during these trips to the Esk that he first saw Cragg Cottage without, of course, having any intimation it could be his future home. 'I remember looking up at it once, at the end of that long pathway on the side of the hill with the fells all around. I remember thinking "the man who lives there must be a happy man".'

It was around this time that Hugh was getting to know a now-famous but then little-known pioneer of stillwater fly fishing, Dr Howard Bell. Although Bell did some of the earliest known work on developing imitations of stillwater nymphs and pupae, he wrote nothing and communicated little of what he did, to others. Hugh met him because Bell had a practice near Blagdon reservoir – a lake Hugh loved and fished regularly when working from the BBC studios in Bristol. Hugh was one of the few people Bell warmed to and would fish with. He was, said Hugh, a rather reclusive man – a brilliant angler but a man scarred, Hugh thought, by appalling experiences in the First World War.

Throughout this time Hugh still flew with the RAF Reserve – and while flying, had another of his periodic brushes with death. He was training a young pilot when the novice froze at the controls and flew the aircraft into the ground. The aircraft was destroyed but both Hugh and the trainee walked away.

In 1950 Hugh began to make documentary films for cinema and television. His first was *Drake's England*. While working on his second, *Shark Island* in 1952, tragedy struck and incredibly Hugh cheated death yet again. Far from land off Ireland's west coast, the small boat he was using hit a reef and went down. The cameraman, a crewman and his new wife of a few months, Diana Vaughan, the young American editor of a literary magazine, were lost. Having tried and failed to save anyone, Hugh swam for eight hours to the shores of Achill Island before being found by fishermen. This time he was the only survivor.

Hugh next married Lady Margaret Vane-Tempest-Stewart, daughter of the seventh Marquess of Londonderry and for some time, while still working, he lived the high life, fishing, shooting, flying and sailing. He was a fiercely competitive sailor and raced against three of the best-known helmsmen of the day, Morgan Giles, Peter Scott and Uffa Fox.

In 1958 this marriage also ended and he married Kathleen Armstrong, the warm, intelligent and down-to-earth lady he stayed with to the end. With the move to 'Cragg' life took on greater stability. His truly productive years began. Hugh made several films for the BBC's Natural History Unit and narrated in his rich and measured voice many programmes made by others.

In the 1960s Hugh formed a long and successful working relationship with Professor Niko Tinbergen, the Nobel Prize-winning specialist in animal behaviour. They made a string of highly successful wildlife films together. *Signals for Survival* (1969) won the Italia Prize and the American Blue Ribbon. *The Gull Watchers, The Sign Readers, The Beachcombers, The Riddle of the Rook* and *The Tender Trap*, a film about carnivorous plants, all found wide international audiences. Two highly personal films followed. In *Salmo the Leaper* Hugh, then in his sixties, astonished viewers by throwing himself fully clothed off a high bank into deep, heavy water to demonstrate how an angler could survive submersion in waders. It was a performance that saved many lives. At one count Hugh had received 17 letters from anglers expressing their gratitude to him. *Self-Portrait of a Happy Man* followed. In 1982 the Royal Geographical Society awarded Hugh the Cherry Kearton Medal for his wildlife work.

There were also, of course, the books. Hugh wrote a number

of wildlife books including *Signals for Survival* (again with Tinbergen); *Nature Detective*, a study of animal tracks and signs; and *The Stolen Years*, a vivid account of his early life. But it will be for his contribution to angling and angling literature, that he is most likely to be remembered.

His most famous book was *Sea Trout Fishing*, first published in 1962 and greatly enlarged in 1975. This was that rarest thing in angling, a wholly original work. Before Hugh, what little had been written about the sea trout had largely been the recycled, received-wisdom kind of stuff that marks so much angling writing. Above all, the fish had been treated by most previous writers as though it fed in freshwater. Not surprisingly, mature sea trout up to that time had been regarded as being virtually uncatchable – by design, at least.

Hugh had long been fascinated by the fish. He had angled for it in Devon as a boy, in Northern Ireland as a serviceman – and in his beloved Esk. When he decided to study it closely he had, as both a naturalist and an angler, the background to begin from first principles. He studied the fish in the sea and in the river; observed that in the sea the fish seemed to feed mostly after dark and quite often in two separate phases; concluded that it did not eat in freshwater but that its feeding responses could consistently be stimulated provided its natural history and in-river behaviour were sufficiently well understood – and then developed an entirely new, coherent, linked and above all effective series of strategies for catching it. *Sea Trout Fishing* covered night fishing and day fishing, river fishing and lake fishing; fishing with sunken line and sunken lure, floating line and floating lure. There were designs for large flies and small flies; notes on lines and leaders, knots and hooks; recipes.

The first edition drew Hugh to wider angling attention, the second created waves that are washing through game fishing still.

Salmon Fishing (1984) was another blockbuster. It did not have the shock-value of its predecessor because it did not come as though a bolt from the blue: the salmon, of course, had been written about for centuries. Yet when this slab of a book arrived from Hugh's mountain eyrie it carried the weight of words written on tablets of stone and was immediately accepted as the definitive work. Among the many ideas and discussions it contained was Hugh's view that no salmon could be overfished provided the angler was sufficiently skilled, and the first theory to make some sense of salmon-taking behaviour, a hypothesis based on hormonal changes within the fish as its time for spawning approaches.

Speycasting appeared in 1994 and set out Hugh's further development of the traditional cast – a variation specifically designed to make use of the lightness and power of carbon fibre. On the way Hugh had collaborated in other books, notably *Freshwater Fishing* (1975) a work of immense scholarship and scope produced with his long-time friend Fred Buller. At the time of his death he was working with Buller on a second book, this time on his only angling hero, Dame Juliana Berners. This author – whether lady or not, no-one is quite sure – published *A Treatyse of Fysshynge wyth an Angle* in 1496. It was the first book on angling in the English language.

All of the books Hugh published had the typical Falkus hallmarks: rigorous appraisal of the field in light of personal experience, clear analysis, lucid argument, copious illustration, meticulous attention to detail and, by the end of each, a wonderful sense of completeness. Together they lifted him to a position of total pre-eminence in the world of salmon and sea trout fishing.

In his later years Hugh had the stature and reputation of an Old Testament prophet. He used his position from time to time to rail against commercialism in angling, against competitive fishing (which he regarded as demeaning for both man and fish), and against the growing practice of catch-and-release because, he argued, it reduced fish to the status of playthings and hence weakened our case in the battle for public opinion.

After his escape from prison camp, Hugh regarded time as the most precious of all life's commodities. His unfinished autobiography was to have been called *Some of it was Fun.*

There is no doubt that Hugh Falkus was to a significant extent shaped by early experiences – by his closeness to his father, a certain distance from his mother, a self-reliance born of his early life in the wide outdoors – and, of course, by his years as a prisoner of war. He was a formidable man: as formidable a man as most men are likely to meet. He did not suffer fools gladly. There is no doubt that he could be crushingly blunt. He could also be bloody-minded and arrogant. He was certainly restless and iconoclastic and in all things fearlessly outspoken. He was in addition, to those he respected and who were in any way close to him, a warm, generous and intensely loyal friend.

Above all in this context, Hugh Falkus was a great man and a great angler. He was an outstanding naturalist and a brilliant communicator. He helped us to understand the world in which we live and the life in the water sweeping past our wading legs. It is not only fishers who owe him a debt.

How to Make Fish Frenzy

At least as much creativity goes into selling to anglers as anglers put into the sport themselves. Fishing writers, who are seen as a link between ambitious marketeers and an innocent public, are bombarded with requests for publicity. Quite often the products and the services offered, are useful. Sometimes they are less so. Some seem as if they have been designed by the lunatic fringe, for the lunatic fringe.

And yet it is rare in fishing for something to be a total loss. Quite often even the daftest or most limited or most inappropriate idea can be turned to advantage. All that is needed is a little flair. Naturally, over the years, I have done my best to provide it. FROM *The Times*, January 21, 1992.

Winter is a depressing time for most anglers. The fly fishing season is still many months away, the coarse fishing season is in the cold-weather doldrums. Dark nights and the chores of fly tying and tackle care, crowd in. It takes pretty good news to cheer the average angler when Christmas has gone.

I propose, therefore, to draw attention to three interesting news items that might have been missed first time around and to reveal my own proposals for following them up. They are proposals which, I am confident, will cheer the most gloom-laden angler, even now.

The first is an announcement from a mail order company. Its

leaflet says that a new Canadian fishing product is to be made available in Britain.

'Fishbuster (TM)' – would I lie? – is a kind of small, plastic vial that is attached to the line near the hook. When bent, the chemicals inside the vial 'glow with a bright green light that draws the fish in like a magnet...

'Fish simply can't resist Fishbuster's deep green fluorescent glow', the Canadian leaflet insists. 'Fishbuster actually lures the closest school right to your line where they frenzy for your bait or lure. All you have to do is keep reeling them in.'

There is a nicely-judged restraint in all of this that will clearly appeal in the English Shires and an injunction to 'use it at the river for trout fishing or salmon' will win over the narrowest of purists on the Test and the Spey. But this is the end of the twentieth century. No trans-Atlantic whizz-bang can be allowed to sweep Europe unchallenged.

It is for this reason that I have developed a rival product of my own, one that exploits a weakness of the Fishbuster by appealing to those who will inevitably become tired of taking simply one fish per cast.

The Greenwell's Grenade (TM) is a fly modelled along the lines of the famous Greenwell's Glory and, indeed, is named after the well-known Church of England Canon who first fired off its dressing 140 years ago.

The Greenwell's Grenade is virtually indistinguishable from its illustrious predecessor and most of the same silks and feathers are used in its dressing. Perhaps the most noticeable difference between the two flies is that whereas Canon Greenwell's creation is simply designed to deceive, my own dressing explodes violently when a trout comes near it.

The trout in question is, of course, lost. Indeed, it is vaporised. But the shock waves are as effective as those produced by a depth charge and bring to the surface for easy netting every other fish within a 30-metre radius. Under favourable conditions, a limit bag of six or eight fish can often be taken with the Greenwell's Grenade in just a couple of casts.

Naturally, the conventions should be observed. A fly as novel and effective as the Greenwell's Grenade cannot be used indiscriminately, no matter how environmentally-friendly the explosives used.

Because of this, no Greenwell's Grenade should be used during the evening rise unless it is smaller than a size 01, long shank. The dry Greenwell's Grenade should only be cast (or in the larger sizes lobbed) upstream on English trout rivers. On the salmon and trout rivers of the North and Scotland, down-and-across is acceptable but not on the redds in the presence of women and children.

The second announcement came in midsummer. A newspaper reported that an 'Ipswich entrepreneur' had successfully gone into business with a slot-machine that dispensed maggots to anglers.

Operating under the catchy slogan 'Bag it with Mag-it', this enterprising gentleman achieved such success with a machine sited on a petrol station forecourt that when last appearing in the angling media he was seeking backers to help him go national.

His small charges were refrigerated to prevent early pupation and, mercifully, were dispensed in cardboard tubes, presumably wriggle-proofed in the manufacturing process.

I am hopeful that the Ipswich entrepreneur and I can team up to market a second product I have developed, one designed specifically to counter the attractions of Fishbuster to the coarse-fishing community. My new Killer Maggots (TM) are tailor-made for the new packaging technology and I expect them to go down a treat.

Killer Maggots are reared on lemming meat and, when thrown into the water as a form of groundbait, will swim in large numbers straight into the mouths of any fish nearby, jamming open their jaws and causing them to suffocate. Naturally, such fish do not fight very well if hooked, but what is lost in performance is more than made up in numbers. Netting them out at the surface, using techniques developed for retrieving trout stunned by the Greenwell's Grenade, is simplicity itself. It goes without saying that Killer Maggots are also environmentally-friendly and may be used with confidence on the purest chalk stream.

The third announcement came from the National Rivers Authority. Its experts said they were convinced that 'fish in shallow and featureless rivers are less happy than those in more varied surroundings'.

I cannot believe it has been necessary to poll even a single roach to unearth this fact. Anglers have long been telling anyone who will listen that fish in rivers of all kinds are unhappy – a fact that many fish seek to indicate themselves by drifting to the surface, dead.

The NRA has a plan to cheer its fish up. It is to sink triangular stone blocks into sections of river to speed up the flow, thus causing 'the erosion of small pools in the bed in which fish like to rest'.

I do not wish to knock this modest proposal, but certainly it falls some way short of a further project I am planning even now. This project is for a series of 'theme' rivers which, like many theme parks, will be modelled on ancient and much-loved legends, the origins of which have been lost in time.

All of my theme rivers will have adequate flows of water, some of it unpolluted. Some will have trees along their banks, others waterfalls and bends and glides, shallows and deeps. There will be curling weedbeds rich with insect life and bright, golden gravels where trout will spawn.

There are some things my rivers will not have. There will be no coin-operated maggot-dispensers on the banks, wriggle-proofed or otherwise. Fishbusters – especially luminous green Fishbusters – will certainly be banned. What is more there will be no need of artificially-installed triangular blocks because my fish will not need cheering up. My fish will be happy as Larry.

So will my anglers. Even in winter. It will make a change.

An Awesome
Experience

There are some places, a few places, that seem in their very names to define raw nature: to conjure images of the primordial, unsullied by man. Alaska is one of them: fang-toothed, snow-encrusted Alaska where grizzlies lumber and red salmon leap and the great bald eagle flies. To fish in such a place, to see an unchanged world as few ever see it, is an awesome experience. FROM *The Sunday Times*, January 29, 1989.

Eight o'clock in the morning and, after a 6.30am call and a gargantuan breakfast, we squeezed ourselves into the tiny float plane: me in my unfamiliar, borrowed chest-waders looking like some deep-sea diver without his helmet; all five of us sweltering beneath long johns, shirts, sweaters, body-warmers, waistcoats, scarves and waterproofs. We knew we had to dress for all weathers and that we would no doubt get them if we gambled on anything else.

'Doors shut? Everyone got a seat belt? OK.'

The pilot adjusted his earphones, the engine fired, we puttered past the other aircraft still loading up – and then the throttle was opened.

Within moments we were juddering and bouncing across the wave-tops, our seats tilted back 30 degrees, the aircraft's nose so high that not even the pilot could see over his controls, and loose hand-ropes beneath each wing gradually neared the horizontal as flying speed was reached. And then an unseen hand slipped beneath us, the vibrations eased, the propeller spun a fleeting cocoon of mist along the fuselage and we banked to starboard behind a headland.

Lift-off: our first day's fly-out over the Bristol Bay watershed of southwestern Alaska, one of the most prolific salmon-breeding grounds left in the world and certainly one of the most remote.

It was the beginning of a remarkable stay at Kulik Lodge, a freckle of spruce cabins on the shores of Nonvianuk Lake. The lodge had four or five aircraft at any one time at the disposal of a dozen and a half anglers. We simply had to decide what we wanted to catch, get up at the alarm call and walk the 50 yards to the shore when we were ready. Everything else was taken care of. There are advantages to being a journalist!

When we had flown in from Anchorage on the 250-mile trip down Cook Inlet the afternoon before, we had seen the Alaska I'd expected.

We had come in low over a true, ice-age wilderness where broken mountains had bared their teeth; where glaciers had gouged and ground; where the high-built peaks of Redoubt and Iliama had risen serene, snowed and outcropped like gigantic chocolate-chip meringues.

But now the wilderness we found below us in the float plane was softer: the lowland Alaska that thaws out for four months of summer, reminiscent of the last week or two of March back home.

Even from the air the tundra looked endless, its coarse grasses and deep-pile mosses unfurling continuously before the horizon. We flew over streams that leapt on horse-back down craggy fells; across vast, contemplating lakes; over small, still lagoons clear as thought itself. Spruce woods were theatrically positioned, almost artistically shaped, growing with a tidiness exaggerated because the sun threw the long, pencil-shading shadows of the trees in the same direction.

It all seemed, from the air at least, a designed kind of emptiness, the kind of wilderness that Capability Brown would have planned.

It took us 20 minutes to reach the thread of broken tinsel we were going to fish. We followed it upstream at about 500ft, navigating by sight the way we had all the way, once banking sharply to our left to see a gigantic brown bear fishing, a vast, rippling fur-mountain bounding and lolloping through the shallows, chasing a frenziedly-turning, zig-zagging V.

We levelled off, banked again to land on a small lake and stampeded a herd of caribou across a patch of snow as we did so.

There was little time for adjustment because the river, as we walked towards it, was hidden by a high bank. One moment we were looking at gently-rising ground, the next scrambling down a steep slope towards a rich red stain in the water.

And then, suddenly, we found ourselves waist-deep in sockeye salmon. The shoal was huge and dense, the fish so inwardly, urgently driven, so oblivious, so many, so close that they were almost disquieting.

Had they been the fresh-minted creatures they had been a couple of weeks before, pouring out of the North Pacific like some endless, silvered, ecological jackpot, it would have been different.

But they were not. These were grotesque fish, caricatures, ravaged by starvation (because salmon do not eat in freshwater) and by the physical changes which the mating cycle brings and which had or would lead to the death of every one. Some had already spawned, some were about to spawn: but always their bodies were a vivid, raw red; their heads olive green, their under-jaws white, their mouths lined with black. Their teeth were elongated and protruding. They had humps on their backs. They did not behave like real fish at all: they were dance-of-death clowns as they splashed and jostled in midstream, pushed and furrowed through the shallows – fins, backs, sometimes even heads and eyes out of water.

Many were dying, a lot dead: tumbling downstream in a ghostly waltz, rolling broadside and log-like in the margins, lying silt-covered in the pools as though moulded in sand; high and dry and stinking on the banks.

We all knew that this was not just happening around us there, but everywhere as far as the eye could see and beyond, for thousands and thousands of Alaskan river miles. We all knew, too, that it was an essential phenomenon – one on which the whole ecology of the region, as well as future generations of sockeye salmon, depended. The scene struck a heart-nerve within us all. Mortality's shroud had stirred and we had glimpsed inside.

It had been an abrupt transition. Lowland Alaska may seem pure Capability Brown from the air, but the wilderness is very real.

There was much else, besides the salmon, to remind us it was real.

There were, for example, the bear stools: low, dark, blueberry-stained mounds along the banks. Every fishing party from Kulik is led by a professional guide and it is because of the bears that every guide goes armed.

The Alaskan brown bear – the grizzly of frontier lore – is the biggest terrestrial flesh-eater in the world. It can stand more than 12ft high, and it lives on everything it can get hold of, from berries to caribou. Normally it is happy to be given plenty of room and right of way by man, but it is unpredictable and nobody takes any chances.

Before our stay was over, we would see such a bear scoop a salmon from the water and strip the briefly-flapping creature clean to its backbone, from gills to tail, in an extraordinarily matter-of-fact way – and then do the same with another fish, moments later.

We would also see several bald eagles wafting by – and two golden eagles together turning on their thermals, making silence. We would see a moose and her calf grazing on a hillside and trip over the dishevelled skeleton of a lone bull in a gully. We would have chirpy ground-squirrels sitting wide-eyed on our bags – and a brown fox so unafraid of man that it would follow us downriver, now and then sitting down interestedly to watch us fish.

We would see, too, our own kind in the wilderness – or in some sort of limbo state between the wilderness and ourselves: Eskimos living beside a river in shacks of wood and corrugated iron. We would see their huskies tethered to stakes around the site as they would be kept all summer, preparing them for the constraints of their traces – and the huge, tent-shaped rack of drying salmon on which they would be fed. We would even see the bruised carcass of a recently killed seal, its guts in a bucket beside it, its smeared skin tossed over a nearby pole like anybody's old coat.

And all of this, all of it – even the volcano craters, steaming and smoking that we circumscribed on a wing-tip, flying so low that we could smell the sulphur – was incidental to what we had gone to do, which was to fish.

And fish we did. All day, every day, intensely.

That first day among the salmon we fished for rainbow trout: our pilot had sought out the salmon because he knew that it was alongside them that the trout would be.

Normally the trout live in the deep lakes through which the rivers flow, lower down: but they follow the salmon up to the head-waters as they swim through the lakes each year, ready to gorge on the pink harvest of eggs when the salmon eventually spawn.

We fished selectively for the trout among the salmon using artificial eggs, because it was eggs that the trout were expecting to see: we used imitation pink eggs, which we fished like flies, from fly-rods.

A tiny split-shot a little way up the line enabled the egg to be drifted close to the bottom where the trout would be looking – salmon eggs are heavier than water – and a tiny piece of coloured polythene a little further up the line helped to indicate a take in the fast, turbulent currents.

And we caught lots: wild, native rainbow trout of a size and in a quantity that would be possible in very few places on earth – and certainly nowhere in Europe.

Always the fight was ferocious, with fish after fish smashing open the surface, splintering the sunlight, sometimes careering so fast and far downstream that I had to follow – running along the bank if I happened to be on it, awkwardly stumbling if I was wading, the rod pulling, the current pushing, my feet groping and tracing, reading the rocks on the bottom like shifting, uncertain Braille. It was a high-wire, electrified day.

Other remarkable days were to follow – for more rainbow trout, for Arctic char and for the three species of salmon still pouring fresh into the Bristol Bay estuaries: pink salmon, chum salmon and cohos.

Some days we were flown to rivers where powerboats had been left so that we could cover mile upon mile of water, stopping at only the best places to catch fish after fish. One day a group of us was flown to a river far inland where an inflatable raft had been dropped – and spent spellbinding hours drifting and fishing across an upland plateau fringed with snow-covered mountains; every detail of the view crackling in air that had the quality of cut crystal.

It is all of these experiences and sensations taken together, of course – the scenery, the wildlife, the fly-outs and the fishing – that give such an adventure its compound magic. But there is in Alaska one thing in addition: the absolute certainty of sport.

Such certainty would not do at all in real, everyday, back-home fishing: it is the roulette of uncertainty, surprise, disappointment and triumph for a given level of skill that lends angling so much of its appeal.

Yet in Alaska, every morning that you and your clothing climb into that cockpit and set off across the wilderness, you know that you are going to get them, by crikey you are going to get them.

It is a certainty experienced while still wide awake, without time or belief needing to be held in suspension.

It is a stolen sensation, illicit in any normal angling context. But once in a while – just once in a while – it is wonderful.

Trout Feeding Behaviour

It is one of the brutalities of the fly fisher's life that 90 per cent of the fish are taken by 10 per cent of the fishermen. Such statistics may be of little concern to beginners, who naturally expect their early results to be modest. For the beginner, everything lies ahead: out there a wide horizon beckons and beyond it, no doubt, remorseless success.

The statistics, though, do not apply to the results achieved by beginners alone: they apply to the results achieved by all anglers. Many of the 90 per cent who are struggling for their share of the 10 per cent are old hands for whom, somehow, things have not clicked.

It is not luck or the weather that consistently makes the difference. Those who succeed do so because they have done what is necessary to bring success. That means, in part, that they have made the effort to observe in a conscious and alert way what is happening before them – and considered what might be learned from what they see.

Nothing a fly fisher sees is more important to him than the behaviour of trout in the water. In Interpreting Riseforms (page 179) I discuss how specific aspects of feeding behaviour can be analysed to give excellent clues to the natural insects the trout might be eating – and hence the best artificials to offer. Here is where that process begins: with an understanding of feeding behaviour in general and what happens when a fish simply swims. FROM *The Times*, May 20, 1994.

T hings are made easier for beginner and old hand alike when the trout are rising. Everyone knows where the fish are because the ebbing rings reveal it. Everyone knows that the fish are in the market for artificial flies because it is the appearance of natural insects on or near the surface that has brought the fish up.

And yet for the angler willing to look closely and think, trout moving at the surface reveal much more than their whereabouts. The riseform each makes can reveal clues so specific to those who can interpret them, that they can turn what otherwise would have been a speculative cast into one of near-surgical precision. That is to say, they can result in a cast fished in the right way, with the right artificial fly. The process will not work in every instance, of course; but it will work often enough to make the unravelling of a riseform's secrets a tool of inestimable value.

When most anglers see a fish rising, they see a generalised disturbance on the water's surface. When the thinking fly fisher sees a rise, he sees the end-product of a process of cause-and-effect. If he has any doubt about what to do, he watches the next rise closely and asks himself three general questions. The first is, how did the water move when the fish rose? The second is – how must the fish have been moving, to cause the water to shift in that way? The third question is – what could have prompted the fish to move in the way that it was?

He asks these questions with an understanding of certain principles, the most important of which is that no creature in the wild expends energy without cause. As a general rule, wild creatures move quickly only when they have to, otherwise they move slowly or not at all. Common sense says this has to be so and everyday observation confirms it. Another general rule is that creatures in the wild will not expend more energy in the pursuit of an item of food than they will replace by consuming it. Again, common sense dictates it: if anything like the opposite applied the fish would get thinner and thinner rather than fatter and more fit. There are many exceptions to both – for example, when there is competition among a group of fish for a particularly desirable food form. But in the main, these two rules are sound enough to form a basis for action.

Because a fish is concerned with enhancing and not depleting its resources, a feeding trout will generally only move quickly when moving to catch something that is itself moving quickly; and if it wants to eat an aquatic snail, it will move at a snail's-pace plus one.

As a consequence, there is often a direct relationship between the movement of a fish and the manner of movement – or the potential for movement – of the creature it wants to eat.

There is also, of course, a direct relationship between the speed of the trout and the force with which it displaces the water around it. If a fish is moving at speed, it will displace water violently – and if this movement occurs at the water's surface, a violent swirl may be seen. If a fish is moving slowly, the water may be displaced hardly at all.

It is on the basis of all of this that the thoughtful angler acts. He will decide tactics and cast knowing that there is likely to be a direct relationship between the movement of the creature the trout is intent upon eating, and the displacement of water – the riseform – that he can see.

Such an awareness is a breakthrough of profound importance for anyone coming to it for the first time. It will bring insights likely to influence his or her entire fishing philosophy. At a stroke the entomological roulette and the wild-eyed rummaging through the fly box become, for much of the time at least, things of the past.

Provided the angler is willing to use his powers of observation and common sense, and is willing to learn a little about the creatures trout eat, the range of possibilities for the insect a given fish is consuming can be significantly narrowed. In certain circumstances, a knowledge of the kinds of insects active at the relevant time of year, at the relevant time of day, on the relevant type of water, and the knowledge of whether or not these insects are large and capable of quick movement, or small and slow can reduce the probabilities to one or two.

Once that stage is reached, the angler is not only able to go straight to the artificial flies most likely to prove effective, but has a built-in understanding of how these flies should be presented and fished. He – or for that matter she – will never look back. The numbers of the 90 per cent who struggle will have been reduced. The ranks of the effective will have been increased by one.

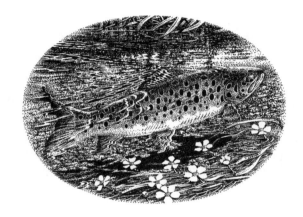

The Breakthrough

So many great minds have applied themselves to fly fishing
that after 2000 years of effort, evolution and not revolution
might seem the natural way forward. Mostly that is what we
have come to expect: a shift of nuance here, the discovery
of another shade of grey there, the development of a minor
tactic that will sometimes work on the second Thursday in
August, but only in a leap year and then if it happens to be
snowing. Anything more is rare. Anything significant is
extremely rare. FROM *The Times*, November 6, 1995.

I have a tip. I think it is a very good tip. It is exactly the kind
of tip my readers have a right to expect from time to time.

This tip – some, I dare say, would call it a breakthrough – is a
simple, confidence-boosting measure which could ease the pressure on difficult days and which could, perhaps, turn what might
have been a blank day into a beano. It has the virtue of being
based on hard-won experience. It came to me recently after two
angling writers, fishing together, had a difficult day.

Apparently – and I had not realised this – some angling writers
do not spend their entire time by the waterside, reeling in whoppers. Some of them – I imagine the number must be very few –
apparently struggle sometimes, like everyone else. And that is
what these two had done. They had spent an entire day, in what
should have been perfect conditions, fishing a well-stocked
reservoir using every trick and tactic fit for the servants to hear
about, catching pretty well nothing. And then, bingo! The penny
dropped and the bright light of insight shone.

The two writers were – well, it doesn't matter who they were;

let us say a friend of mine and his friend.

When we – which is to say, they – arrived at the water one autumn day, it was wondrously still. Martins dipped and scooped. Here and there trout dimpled the surface. From time to time a violent swirl showed a great fish in the margins. Light cloud and a breeze were promised for later. After that, calm and with it, no doubt, the inevitable evening rise. It was going to be a doddle. Jammy, they called it.

At 10.00am, they started. Being angling writers and having lots of books and hundreds of articles behind them, they knew exactly what to do. They would fish the shallower water, because that was where the fish would be gathering in autumn, and they would each use different tactics to double their chances. Doubling their chances is just the kind of thing angling writers think about. My friend put on a dry fly and, because there was so little drift, his friend decided to fish small nymphs close to the bottom. The pair wanted to take their limits – their first limits, anyway, before buying their second tickets – entirely on light lines and small flies if they could.

By 10.30am, nothing. By 11.00am, nothing. My friend began to change fly patterns and sizes and colours. His friend began to fish his nymphs in mid-water and then just under the surface. They both lengthened their leaders in case the fish were being scared by the lines.

At 11.30am they moved into deeper water, working out – again, this is the kind of thing fishing writers do – that the sun must be keeping the trout in the cooler deeps a little longer than expected. There was no wind and they did not drift much. At around noon, the water erupted very close to the place they had left. Tiny fry leapt into the air.

Naturally, my friend was ready. He knew all about fryfeeders and the way big trout gorged in the autumn, fattening up for winter. He had a special rod already prepared and a fly which suggested a small fish wonderfully well.

Swish, swoosh, my friend's rod went and the fly landed perfectly where the swirls had been. Swish, swoosh, he went again and again. In fact, he swished and swooshed quite a bit before the swirls stopped and the boat moved on.

At 1.30pm they pulled into the bank for lunch. They noticed that everyone else kept on fishing and saw, now and then, splashes around outstretched nets.

'Anyone who will fish through his lunch hour is just a fishmonger', my friend's friend said. 'No appreciation of the view. No interest in the wildlife.'

'Pathetic', my friend replied – just before a couple of nice fish rose along the bank and he tried to run towards them in a nonchalant, unconcerned kind of way, before tripping in his wellies and falling headlong.

Around 3.00pm the promised breeze sprang up and a nice ripple pleated the surface. The promised cloud came, too, but it made no difference.

At 4.30pm my friend's friend switched to a sinking line and a lure the size of a parrot. 'I hate doing it, but sometimes it's the only way', my friend's friend said.

'Sometimes it is the only way', my friend concurred.

It seemed to get hotter after that and then insufferably hot. The two friends gradually became testy and apparently a few sharp words were exchanged. The hours ticked painfully by.

Just after 7.00pm my friend, who has written all manner of books and articles and told countless fly fishers how to take trout in all manner of conditions with ease, got a tangle. 'Oh, look, I've got a tangle', he said. Something like that. 'It's a long drive. I'm going to knock off.'

'All right', said his friend, who has also written all manner of books and articles and told countless fly fishers how to succeed in all manner of conditions, 'I'll just have one last cast.'

For a couple of minutes his fly rode the soft swell and then my friend's friend called it quits and began to reel in. Not far from the boat there was a tremendous swirl, a great trout took and my friend's friend was startled almost out of his wits.

'You should have done that earlier', my friend said as he netted the fish. 'If you'd had your last cast earlier you'd have had plenty of time to come and then you might have caught a lot more.'

'What a brilliant idea', his friend replied. 'If you have your last cast early and get a fish, you could go on from there and maybe get a few. You could even have your last cast first and get a bagful. What a wonderful tip!'

'Could be a breakthrough', my friend replied.

'Revolutionary', my friend's friend said.

Finding Trout on Lakes

Finding the fish on big lakes like Grafham, Rutland and Chew is the greatest challenge in fishing them. Most blanks come because the water fished contained few or no trout. Even though every water has its hot spots these may not be known to the casual angler and, if known, may well be occupied by the time he arrives.

So where is the occasional visitor to begin? There are no certainties. The time of year and the weather on the day can stand the experience of the last visit on its head. But still there are some rules of thumb. FROM *The Times*, May 6, 1994.

Large lakes, especially the big reservoirs, can be daunting places when no fish are rising. There can often appear to be so much featureless water, so many places where the fish might not be, that whole weeks could be spent in prayer and speculation.

Even so there are many clues to the places where, on a given day, trout might be gathered. The topography of the surrounding land, the wind and the water temperature hold the keys. The basic notion is, find the food, find the fish.

Most of the food that trout eat will be found in water less than 15ft deep – and much of that will be in water less than 10ft deep. For water 10ft or deeper to be within casting distance for an angler fishing from the shore, the lake bed will have to fall away quite steeply.

A steeply-sloping bank is a good, though not infallible,

indicator of a steeply-sloping lake bed – and also, as it happens, of a place that has not been disturbed by wading anglers. Consider also, if there is one, a dam wall. Dam walls are not aesthetic places but they slope steeply beneath the water and are likely to hold fish within casting distance all season. They can be wonderful places with the wind blowing onto them – especially a wind that has been sustained for some time, in summer.

A wind affects the water, the fish and their food in several ways. It pushes the top layer of water along above the slower-moving (but never static) layer beneath – and moves any insects held in it, also. A wind oxygenates the water which, on dull, warm days is likely to encourage the fish to the surface. It also causes ripples and waves, that help to disguise the angler and his line.

In warm weather, a wind also cools the water and, if it has been blowing from the same direction for long, it piles all this oxygenated, cooler, food-rich water onto the downwind bank. This is where the best fishing will be because the trout will be there. Fishing a downwind bank from a boat is no problem because the casting is with the wind. Fishing it from the shore can be tricky because every cast is into the gusts.

A promontory is a fine place if it has deep water around it. Even if it has water only a couple of feet deep around it, that is the place to be when a wind is blowing across the point. This wind is pushing a conveyor-belt of new water containing both food and fish that would otherwise be out of reach, within casting distance.

Indeed, two of the most memorable days I had on the big lakes were in such shallow water. On Draycote I once took eight fish from the bank in 90 minutes by casting midge pupae into water maybe knee-deep. I took another bag on Rutland fishing so close in that I was casting amid weeds and bankside debris that broke the surface. The water there was two feet deep or less and the fish, brought in by the wind and finding the place up to that point undisturbed because it was so difficult to fish, were feeding on the nymphs, larvae and snails which abounded there. The boat was almost grounding but, casting just off the bank and between the visible snags, my companion and I took a bagful.

While deep water is commonly the most productive – trout can often be spooky in the shallows, especially if there are wading anglers about – any bankside features' that provide cover and promote the growth or accessibility of food will attract trout.

Old hedgerows growing down into the water or submerged trees rising up from it are well-known standbys. So are the mouths of incoming streams. Streams bring added food into a lake and can also raise or lower temperatures in the lake near them in a helpful way. Late in the season trout gather off the mouths of incoming streams because they are programmed to run up them to spawn.

The boat angler has access to all of these places and to some others.

Boat anglers soon become familiar with wind lanes on the water. These curious, long reaches of calm in a lake that is other-wise rippled, are marvellous fish attractors: the thicker surface film on calm water makes it more difficult for insects swimming up to it, to break through and hatch. Trapped insects mean easy pickings and the trout know it. With seemingly fishless water all around, trout can be seen moving up and down these lanes, often with their backs out of the water and their dorsal and tail fins catching the light.

For all their seeming preoccupation such fish should be approached with caution. If the nerves are strong enough and fish are approaching, it is better to lie in wait and ambush them. But given that they can and often do turn back and go the other way, or disappear altogether, it can take an iron man to do it.

Birds flying low over the water, or spiralling high above it, can indicate a hatch of fly from a distance. Any hint of a distant fly hatch should be investigated. Fly hatches attract hungry trout.

There is one other feature that it is worth the boat angler looking for and worth learning how to relocate: the shallow area far out in otherwise deep water.

Any shallows in the middle of a lake that rise to within less than 15ft of the surface are likely to have fish over them much of the time. Some of the big reservoirs have bars that come to within a rod's length of the surface in summer but a long way from the shore, with seemingly no clear markers, they can be difficult to find again once the boat has drifted over and left them far behind. The same is true, of course, of a shoal of feeding trout far out from the bank. Once a fish or two has been taken from a particular spot, it pays to go over the same place time and again – if only it can be found.

There is a wrinkle, here. Any fixed point in a lake – though shoals of trout do have an unreasonable habit of moving – can be relocated at will. All that is necessary is to line up two points on the bank ahead and two to one side when a fish is being played or an area of shallower water is found amid deep. Thereafter, whenever these two sets of references have again been brought in line together, the boat is where it was when the first sightings were made.

Here endeth the broad rules of thumb. Rules of thumb are all they are. There is only one golden rule and that is, keep moving if nothing is seen or caught. Most days, alone on the bank, an hour is quite long enough to test out one spot. For two anglers in a boat, each using different techniques and exploring different depths, a lot less will usually do.

Even on the likes of Grafham, Rutland and Chew, the fish have to be somewhere.

A Fly Fishing Club

Many anglers buy fishing books. One of my own favourites
is *Where the Bright Waters Meet*, by Harry Plunket Greene.
It is the story of the author's years in a small fishing club on
a small stream in the early part of this century. It is an uplift-
ing book, a joyous read. I once belonged to such a club. It
was on my local river, not far from the great man's own. It
was of a similar size and run on similar lines. The members
seem to have been similar, too.

T he stream winds in that place through a hidden valley. The
only approach is along a narrow, gravelled drive that runs past
the landowner's house and threads its way through his grounds.
It is an amazing thing simply to go up that drive. It leads off a
road on the edge of a town. Here is the real world, all bustle and
noise, there is the drive sandwiched between two buildings. You
turn in. After a hundred metres or so the buildings end, the drive
takes a sharp S-bend and there, as though the rest had been a
screen suddenly drawn aside, is the valley. There is not a building
nor a person nor a machine in sight, there is nothing that is not
lovely to intrude. There is only sliding water and green meadows
and trees and wild flowers; maybe a few sheep and cows; a low,
protecting hill and some enclosing woods.

The valley is on the edge of the town and yet the entrance is
so unlikely and secure, the valley so cloistered and shawled that
some of us wondered whether the locals knew it was there or, at
least, knew quite what was there.

Even if the local poachers had known, and of course, they did
know, they could not have reached the water we fished. The river

untangled itself at the head of the valley, then wound over the flat land like unravelled braid. There were many strands. We had the central strand, the main river which imaginatively we called The Main. We also had a short thread of water which we called The Carrier. There was another carrier between ours and the town. The trees and bushes along that carrier had been allowed to grow wild as both a barrier and a screen. That water was unfishable. There were other threads of water beyond much of The Main and so mostly we fished from islands between islands. In all the years I was there I only once ever saw strangers on the banks and that was on a baking day when a couple of lads and their girls had swum there. That is how secret and secure it was.

The water became ever-more clear as the year advanced. It was full of ranunculus. In May and June, in full flower, the long tresses streamed and curled like drowned hair, the white flowers offered up could have been a daisy meadow winding. The weed was a jelly of life. There were olive nymphs, shrimps, caddis, snails, simulium, you name it. Between the weeds, in the racing channels and under the banks, trout; usually, somewhere, even on the worst day, one rising if you looked hard enough.

The land between the streams was rough meadow. It can never have seen a fertiliser or an insecticide or a plough. It was low ground, coarse-tussocked, cut about with ancient drainage channels long-since silted and overgrown. Fence posts as grey and loose as old bones gangled along the ditches and here and there on the rusted, drooping wire the clicked wool of a stray sheep hung. In one place, by a planked footbridge, a spring welled up. It burgeoned, lifting domes of soft light, like water-flowers blooming. The stream and the carrier were fringed with branched burr-reed and brooklime, meadowsweet and hemp agrimony, purple loosestrife and yellow flag. There were coots and moorhens, swans and ducks, lapwing and snipe. Kingfishers put blue splinters in the eye.

The fishing hut was on the banks of the carrier facing the hill to the west. The hill was covered in woods and many herons nested high in the beeches. In the mornings, if the wind was right, the birds simply bent their wings over curves of air and slid down them to the shallows. It was not uncommon to catch trout that had been too heavy for a heron to lift. They were stabbed clean through.

The fishing hut was the centre of this small universe. It was long and low, brick-built, slate-roofed, covered in Virginia creeper that one of the members, a lovely man now long gone, had planted.

The hut had once been a pigsty and that suited us fine. The inside walls were painted white. There were a few old scuffed carpets and rugs that were bound to the bare concrete floor by decades of wellie-mud, a long table that would seat all of us, a few old dining chairs that were so hollow in the seat that they hurt the bum. There were, dotted here and there, huge, decrepit armchairs that had kapok stuffing poking out of small holes, like white mice escaping.

At one end of the hut there was a huge wrought-iron fireplace where, in autumn and winter, we made terrifying log fires that sometimes forced us back as far as we could go, blotched and mottled. The fire had a huge hood over the grate that had originally, someone said, been the hood of a chip shop fryer. It was a wonderful hood except that it was not very functional. Whenever the fire was on smoke billowed around all three sides, kippering everyone. Nobody complained. We simply sat there talking, eating and drinking in the fug. 'Anyone mind if I have a cigar?' a visitor once asked. 'Say nothing', an old hand replied, 'no-one will notice.'

It was a wonderful, homely place to gather but it was the people who made the club.

There were only 15 of us, 12 men and three women plus wives and husbands who were greatly encouraged. We were less a fishing club, more a social club where some fishing was done, not all of it serious. We were a mixed bunch, hand-picked. No-one ever applied. The choosing of members was as mysterious a process as the choosing of Popes. D, the landowner, made the decision alone and always got it right. One imagined the fire blazing, the high chimney smoking, the round-robin written to the smell of incense burning, the joyous peeling of bells. '*Habemus member.*'

First, the telephone rang. It was the same for us all. The telephone rang and a general interest was elicited and then an invitation to 'come and see the water' followed. Nobody was fooled. We were looking at the water, D was looking at us. The only question was, would we 'fit in'. D, benign but shrewd, could pick and choose. The fees in those early days were not great. I had many friends who paid more for a rod on a local still-water than we paid to fish that wonderful river in that wonderful place. Profit was not in it. D wanted the management of the river covered and congenial people around.

We all knew that it was unreal, that it could not last. We all knew we were fishing on borrowed time. We often talked about it.

There were no club rules. I did once suggest, late one evening, that we institute a couple, just to show willing. 'No wading above the nose' was one, I remember. 'Nothing to be caught' was another suggestion. Others chipped in with helpful ideas of their own. I seem to remember we produced a fine list of rules and that there was general acceptance of these sensible suggestions, but they were never written down and so never achieved the force of law. I expect they would have been broken, anyway.

We were all sorts – an insurance salesman, a couple of doctors, a couple of lawyers, an estate agent, a few businessmen, a retired schoolteacher, a brace of retired lieutenant-colonels; me.

I got the place that E had vacated by dying. That is rather the way it was. I never met E but he must have been a great character. He had been 90 or close to it, wore shorts and he wobbled up the drive on a bicycle with half a dozen rods poking out every-where, already made up. He came with the rods already made up because he had to. E could not rely on finding another member on the water and could hardly see to tie on his flies so everything had to be prepared at home. He must have looked like a porcu-pine on wheels. On fishing days he must have cut swathes through the town, there must have been chaos behind him. E always fished the same 50 yards of water. He caught little but enjoyed himself immensely. What else was to matter?

At one time the club had been run rather formally, on a beat system. Mercifully that ended before I joined. By the time I got there everyone was just mucking in. More times than not you had the place to yourself, every now and then there would be a hatch of members. Sometimes we wandered the whole water in twos and threes, talking, laughing, taking the fishing in turns. Sometimes, as the mood mutually struck us, we gave one another plenty of room so that we could get on with the business in hand. It was all done by instinct and ether, but mostly we got it right.

Every part of the water had a name. There was this bend, that bend, the other bend. There was so-and-so's point, somebody else's seat, somebody else's meadow, that hole. There was the island. Of course, we had Water's Meet.

The fishing when we did it – and do not let me deceive, we did sometimes fish, sometimes intently – could be fascinating. In truth, the fish on the Main bends were some of the trickiest I have met anywhere. The river on the bends was heavy and fast. It had sculpted deeps and shallows and had gouged out the banks. Great weedbeds grew. The surface was puckered and pleated with currents and counter-currents. Drag, the need to defeat drag, was the name of the game.

I remember my first brace well. I caught it on my second visit, quite late in April, quite late in the evening. The fish rose hard into the near bank on so-and-so's point. They made subliminal rises, each small disturbance instantly teased out and destroyed by the current. Somehow I got a fly to them both, without drag. First cast, a wild brown trout of 2lbs 13oz. Second cast ditto, 2lbs 14oz. I killed them both. I do not know why, but I did, even though I was quite alone. Maybe it was something of the ancient hunter coming out, a mental need to leave my mark on this new territory. I do not know. In the 13 years that followed I did not kill another wild trout from that water. We are odd creatures.

Every month was wonderful, but May was most wonderful. We had the grannom and the hawthorn and the mayfly. I loved mayfly time. The mayflies hatched in precisely the right numbers:

always enough to bring up the biggest fish and keep them interested, never enough to allow the trout to gorge and go down.

It was the same most mayfly days. We were all of us waiting by mid-afternoon – the swifts and martins quartering the river on urgent, slippery wings; the ducks and the coots and the waterhens in the sheltered places, the trout restless and urgent on the fin: my friends and me. The spiders.

The hatch could start in any way. Sometimes we would see a heavy swirl in the current, sometimes we saw a fly on the wing, once I saw two translucent wings flutter to the ground after a bird had snipped out the body between them. Then, suddenly, the full hatch would come on and time seemed to happen all at once. The rest of the day dissolved into a purring symphony of winking light, swaying weed, rising trout, bending rods and forever mayflies fluttering upwards. Through it all the wild flowers gleamed and the cuckoos called and the bells of the parish church peeled to remind us this was heaven.

Summer evenings were different and yet in many ways much the same. The sedges scuttered and the trout swirled, the spinners crucified themselves and the trout sipped. Later we sat outside the hut under the winking stars, talking softly while the rosewater carrier flowed past our feet and we looked towards the hill and the recently-set sun. The bats flickered like bow ties on the gloaming, the ducks in the reeds made low conversation, the swans sailed in single file upstream as though escorts to some barge of state. Often the barn owl would hawk the meadows and we would see him drop like a lead pillow falling.

There were many incidents. JJ's first meeting with my three young daughters – 'come on, team' – and away he went with them running behind him, for all the world like a Pied Piper in breeks. There was Vanessa's first fish, a 2lb brown caught on one of the first flies she tied. There was J's 18lb salmon caught on a fly, A's 18lb pike, caught on a goldfish, T's stirring battle with the heifer hooked on his backcast, my big grayling.

There was the sombre reality of the morning my doctor friend arrived and I said he looked tired and he said yes, he had been up much of the night holding an old man's hand while he died.

He would not have mentioned it had I made no comment because that is the way his world is. And then we fished on through another day with the clover out and skylarks singing just as the pair of us had previously arranged.

There was the distinguished lawyer I found peering at a note that D had pinned up. Someone new had left an aromatic bag of litter in the hut. The note was typically brief and wry. 'There is no refuse collection service from the hut.' The distinguished lawyer scrutinised it over the top of his half-eyes and rubbed his head as though seeking weevils in some complex contract or trying to interpret a tricky piece of law.

'How do *you* read that, Brian? I mean, how do you *read* it?'

'Take your litter home.'

A pause. 'Oh. Ah. Yes, yes.' The famous head beginning to nod, the slow light dawning.

There were the hilariously-captioned photographs on the noticeboard, the magazine cuttings about this and that, the occasional note left ostensibly to one member with the express intention of amusing the rest. There were the labelled finds that led to correspondence – memorably the labelled egg.

The swan's egg was left in the hut one day with a note beside it. 'This swan's egg was found in the carrier at X', the note said. Every time I went in for weeks after, someone had added a comment. First, 'This cannot possibly be a swan's egg. Swans do not lay their eggs in the water. I suspect that this is the egg of the Pale Watery.' Beneath that, 'Mr X may know a lot about business but he knows nothing about entomology. This egg cannot possibly have come from a Pale Watery. It is the wrong colour.' And then, 'This correspondence is becoming ridiculous. Mr Y has noticed the egg's colour but has failed to notice its size. It is far too big to have been laid by a Pale Watery. This egg has to be from the Exceedingly Large Dark Olive.' And so on, all the while the huge object slowly beginning to fester and smell in the heat and nobody wanting to remove it because that would end the correspondence and the fun.

Eventually, of course, there came the signs and omens. After so many years, so many days, so many fish, so many jolly lunches, so many impromptu parties, so many happy nights that ended in the procession of cars that scrunched and rolled down the pot-holed drive to a real world long forgotten and then suddenly resurrected in the stabbing lights, they had to come. A new regime. First prices doubled, then they trebled. Not everyone in the club could afford them. Other small changes here and there. One by one we began to drift away.

There was sadness but no resentment at what was done. That is the way the real world goes. We had all known it could not last. We had all known we had been fishing on borrowed time. We had often talked about it.

A Rude Awakening

The young angler's mind is an adhesive thing. Anything to do with fish and fishing can stick. Anything that touches on great fish – especially great fish in unreachable waters – can implant images that become more vivid and powerful with each passing year. By adulthood a young angler's memory can become a fantasy which must, if the opportunity occurs, be lived out. I once went back and fished out a fantasy. I found that one aspect of it had changed somewhat. I also found a dream that had turned into a nightmare. FROM *The Sunday Times*, January 27, 1991.

Ever since, as a boy, I had peered over the bridge in Galway City and had looked down into the Corrib River, I had wanted to fish there.

I had eyes, of course, only for the salmon, taut and flexing, sidling and drifting, hard on the bottom in the clean, sleeking water. They were grey-helmeted, visored, on metabolic auto; fuelled only by the urge to drive upstream and mate, by the need to play out their destinies in the thin light of the redds.

Going back, doing it for just one afternoon in a week-long break, had seemed such a good idea, 30-odd years on.

'A Condom. I got it on a Flying Condom.' He was standing high on a catwalk that bordered the wall alongside the river, holding the small grilse triumphantly aloft with one hand, jiggling in the other what I knew, though I could not make it out, to be the salmon lure of that name. It was a rude awakening in more senses than one.

I was waist-deep in chest-waders, fulfilling my dream, wielding

an unfamiliar, double-handed fly-rod just downstream from the
thin spillage of water that was being allowed into the parched
river from the weir.

Downstream, to my right, the grey-stone, green-domed
Cathedral of Our Lady and St Nicholas loomed above the
skyline, marooned on its island amid a constant encirclement of
traffic and tourists. To my left, the square tower and grey stone
façade of St Vincent's Convent of Mercy provided a com-
positional balance.

Spanning the river between them, directly below me, was the
bridge over which I'd peered as a boy: the bridge over which that
day, in shifts, it seemed the entire population of the city took
turns to gaze. There were local folk with shopping, old men with
pipes, several troupes of colourful youngsters who mostly
seemed to be German; there were boys in shirt sleeves, women
in dresses, a few pessimists wearing anoraks and once, away to my
left, there was a brief flap of nuns.

'I can lend you one if you like. I said I can lend you a
Condom.' The man on the catwalk was still trying to help, his
voice curiously clear above the noise of the traffic and the easing
of the water, shattering again the cocoon of concentration that,
for a few moments at least, had held the salmon and me so intimately and close.

'A bit to the left. You need to be a bit to the left.' — a new
voice, this time, someone on the bridge being insistently helpful,
telling me where my fly should be to cover a fish. The caller
hitched himself further over the bridge wall, reached down an
arm, pointed a finger. 'They're here. The salmon are right here.
One of them's enormous.'

A double-deck bus went by, touring heads craned, there was
the brief, futile pop of a flashgun from behind a window and it
was gone, bearing away a lady and her picture of nothing but
reflected light.

A child's lollipop fell into the water. There was more craning
of heads, a reaching down of arms, a pointing of fingers. Tears.
And then my line, caught in an updraught of wind from beneath
the bridge, touched the rod-tip and manufactured a form of

aerialised spaghetti that collapsed all around me.

The heroic salmon faded again. This was not the stuff my dreams had been made of, not quite how I'd imagined it all those years ago. Then I'd seen only the fish. Now I had a wider view. Going back, doing it, was proving a qualified experience.

I would not want to give a false impression. The Weir Pool on the Corrib River in Galway City is one of the great salmon pools in Ireland and it is fine fly water. I had simply caught it between runs. The fish that lay in the low, warm water below me that day had their minds only on the redds and on survival. They had seen a thousand flies and were not going to take mine.

But at the right time of year (which is to say of my salmon fishing, at any other time of year) a score of salmon can be caught there in a day.

At those times the crowds will fade, the traffic subside, the buildings move back. Then only the electrified line will be real: the line and the fly and the fish.

Even without fish, there is a curious normality about fishing for salmon in the middle of an Irish city. The experience, for angler and audience both, is wholly consistent with the place of angling in the community. No country that I have ever fished in takes its fishing so seriously. In no country that I have ever visited is angling a more normal part of life.

This is especially so in Connemara, where we travelled next. There, everything proclaims the place of angling as an everyday pursuit. Like going to work. Or the races.

'Joe Whelan – Butcher, Hardware, Fishing Tackle'; 'Murphy's Tea Rooms – Souvenirs, Postcards, Fishing Tackle, Vegetables'; 'Dolan: Fishing Tackle, Groceries, Cycles Repaired'. And the signposts – 'Brown Trout Fishing 2 Miles'; 'To the Salmon Leap'; 'Tackle, boats for hire, 200 yards'.

And, of course, there is the angling in the pubs. Pubs, everywhere, live and breath it. 'Jaez you should have seen the fish I lost last night' ... 'Took a Peter by the Big Rock' ... 'Salmon? Call that a salmon? Listen, I'll tell you about a salmon ...'

Images from everywhere roll and dissolve, merge into one. The smoke from the peat fire in the cottage near Ballinrobe, gently kippering us as we sat up late; the pyramid of turf turning amber, then white; settling like old bones; collapsing. There was the ritual of the Guinness at Leenane, the last of the sun touching the Maamturk Mountains, the round, mute moon above Kylmore Abbey. There was the silver of the lake near Clifden, the flicker of bats, the audible slurps of the trout near Cong, sipping in drowned flies on a Bible-black night.

For all the delights of the trip, however, it was a pilgrimage tinged with gloom, the terrible, jarring message being brought home to me more sharply than anywhere on the Errif, below Aasleagh Falls.

It was on the Errif, in 1975, that I took the first salmon of my life. It fell – it was one of the joyous checks and balances of a sport that can so often disappoint – to a fly of my own design and tying within an hour of reaching the water, in a drought. It was on the Errif, also below the falls, that I caught my first sea trout the same day. Ever since, in my mind, Ireland has seemed symbolised by these two wonderful fish.

Well, there are still salmon on the Errif, but there are precious few sea trout. In fact, there are precious few sea trout anywhere in Connemara, from Achill Head in the North to Galway Bay in the South.

The sea trout that once spilled into the rivers like some silvered, ecological jackpot, making arrowheads through the shallows, swimming up the falls, leaping and cavorting in the pools, have suffered a disaster. The runs even on the most famous fisheries – the Errif, Delphi, Burrishoole, Ballynahinch, Costelloe – are catastrophically down, reduced from thousands a year to in some cases hundreds and tens, even singles.

Emotions have run high because so many are affected and so much is at stake. Connemara has many anglers of its own. Many hotels and ghillies live by angling tourism and many touring anglers want trout. Livelihoods are being lost, businesses are threatened.

A host of reasons has been mooted for the decline and collectively they may all be making a contribution, as they are in Scotland and the other places where migratory fishes run:

afforestation (which can increase the acidity of the tiny streams in which the sea trout breed), peat harvesting and sheep grazing (which can tip silt into the water, clogging the spawning redds), drainage schemes (which increase water velocity), silage-making (which can poison water) and so on.

But the central reason seems to be the huge growth of salmon farming in the coastal bays and estuaries.

The group which is fighting the cause of the angler argues that the farms mean many more hosts are available to sea lice, one species of which is specific to salmon and sea trout. In response to the presence of more host fish, they say, the sea lice populations have exploded – only to be driven away from the fish cages by chemicals poured over them for that very purpose.

Having lost one host a louse must find another quickly or die. Sea trout smolts have to swim close to the salmon cages on their way from rivers to the sea. In the sea, they stay conveniently close to the shore. In the desperate struggle of all life to survive, dozens, hundreds of lice are attaching themselves to each young fish on the way out and to the larger fish on their way back. The fish are being eaten alive. I have seen the appalling photographs for myself.

The argument has raged for years while science and politics establish different truths and vested interests on all sides fight to hold what they have. In the meantime the marvellous, volatile, acrobatic sea trout get fewer and fewer.

I only realised how bad things were near the end of the trip: And while it had been an amusing highlight to fish that bright afternoon in Galway City, it was profoundly sad to drift a famous lough on a perfect day, casting over water I came to realise was near-empty.

It was like fishing for ghosts.

Where Trout Lie
in Rivers

One of the more extraordinary moments I have experienced on a river was when I was fishing a dense hatch of mayfly. The air was thick with flies. They hazed the light. The water was carpeted. Everywhere, trout were rising. It was, moving slowly upstream, almost a fish a cast.

I do not know how many fish I had taken up to that point, but on a bend I met an angler on my own bank, coming downstream. He looked frustrated. I asked him how things were going. 'Terrible', he replied. 'Haven't had a thing. What about you?'

'Oh, a few', I replied, lifting into another. 'One or two.'

'What are you getting them on?' he asked, waving his arms about to keep the insects from his face. 'I've been using something small and black and that's useless.'

Of course, I helped him at once – but that is a perfectly true story. Even long-time anglers can ignore, or be unaware of, evidence of what is happening all around them, in the air and on the water.

Some of the most helpful evidence a river offers – hatch or no hatch – is where fish are likely to be, even when none are rising. Some reaches are crammed with trout, others are bare. It is by no means uncommon for an angler at a given point on a bank to bemoan his lack of 'luck' while casting repeatedly over water where no fish could possibly be.

It does not have to be that way. Clues are everywhere. Here are some of them. FROM *The Guardian*, May 5, 1990.

WhEN the average person looks at a river, he sees a stretch of water sliding and rumpling between two banks: a place to walk the dog by, or wax romantic or, heaven help us, swim.

He is aware that the width and depth change here and there; that there are bends and straight reaches; that sometimes the banks have trees close to the water's edge and that other banks are bare; that in places the river bottom is covered with clean stones and gravel – and elsewhere it is clouded by silt and mud; and that in certain spots the surface is broken by weedbeds or submerged logs or pilings.

What he may not know – and what surprisingly few anglers realise – is the extent to which all of these features are like symbols on a map. They can be 'read' or interpreted to provide a vivid picture of what is happening not only to the river itself but to the life within it.

While an ability to 'read the river' is vital for all serious fishermen, the skill is for no-one more important than it is for the fly fisher seeking trout. For any fly fisherman, the most electrifying cast is that to a specific fish. The ability to 'read' the river – to look at the water and know where fish will be and what they are likely to be doing – provides opportunities to cast to trout with great precision, even when no fish can be seen.

Three factors dominate the life of the trout, as they do the lives of most other creatures in the wild: the need of food, the need of security and the need to conserve energy. Where a reach of a trout stream provides all three together, then there the fish will be.

The interpretive process begins with food, without which no fish at all will be present.

Some of the trout's food – mostly insects – can be acquired from the riverbed: but a large part of it is carried towards the fish on the current.

Because one of the needs of the fish is to conserve energy, it will seek out places where most food is carried; in other words, where it will get the maximum return of food for the minimum expenditure of effort. That means places where currents and eddies gather in food from a wide area and funnel it into a narrow, dense concentration.

However – again like most wild creatures – the trout is wary of predators and danger. It feels safest when it is lying in or alongside deep water, into which it can sink like a dimly remembered dream at the first hint of a shadow falling across it, or the flash of reflected sunlight from a highly-varnished rod.

An excellent place to expect trout to be is where a broad current is funnelled into a narrow one, either over deep water or immediately alongside deep water. And if overhead cover and shade are available, too, then the trout is at its happiest, is most secure – and is most vulnerable to the angler with the ability to place his fly where he wants it to go.

Several features can create currents which funnel food from a wide area into a narrow stream and can cause deep sections of water to be created. The most important are bends in the river, objects projecting up from the bottom or out from the banks, and incoming sidestreams.

By and large, most of the trout on bends will be found along the outside bank, with the inside of the bend usually being shallow and often silted up and fishless. This is because on bends the main flow of the river (and the vast bulk of the food it carries) pushes into the outside bank. What is more, the constant weight of water hitting that bank will eat into it, gouging out not only the bankside but the riverbed, creating a channel of deeper water, close in. Where such bends have a significant flow of water and also are blessed with overhanging trees, then good trout for that river will live.

Similar funnellings and gougings are also created in miniature in the main flow of an otherwise apparently straight piece of water by rocks or gravelbeds on the bottom, by weedbeds, by piling from old bridges (or existing bridges which also provide cover), by trees fallen into the water and by many other objects besides.

Often such objects provide a second service to trout: they break the full force of the current and cause a stable 'pad' or cushion of slowed water on their upstream sides, in which the trout can lie with very little expenditure of energy. Even in fast water, fish in clear streams can be seen to lie in front of rocks and weedbeds and the like, holding position with only the merest twinkling and fanning of their tails.

It is for this reason that the upstream sides of small waterfalls or 'sills' should be given particular attention. They are, of course, formed by a line of stones or other objects which, just below the surface, hold the water back – and so there is a hospitable cushion of water for the trout to ride, right across the river.

Inflowing sidestreams add attractions of their own to what might otherwise be straight and uninteresting reaches. They introduce an additional flow of food into the main river and also cut a deeper channel into the bed of the river which trout (and many other species of fish) find attractive.

Quite apart from the clues which the river provides, trout can also physically betray their presence even when they are not rising, or otherwise breaking the water's surface. Sometimes, for example, small puffs and clouds of silt can be seen drifting down an otherwise clear stream – and often the cause can be traced back upstream to a fish rummaging head-down in a weedbed to dislodge nymphs and insect larvae.

More interestingly, large individual fish which stay in a lie for a long time can, through their constant movements and closeness to the bottom, clean small areas of silt or algae from an otherwise dark riverbed. The result can be a light patch on the riverbed which, on a bright day, can heliograph the whereabouts of a fish from 50 yards away.

Not all light patches on the bottom, of course, are caused directly by the movements of fish: the majority are created by localised turbulences around rocks and over depressions. But here again, the proximity of fish is likely because such smaller turbulences, as well as cleaning areas of the river bottom, can also funnel and concentrate food. As a consequence, fish tend to hang about near them. I have personally observed trout moving from one light patch to another, in regular succession, in a seemingly restless, hunting manner – perhaps actively looking for concentrated food.

All of the above points are hints and clues on how to read a river; how to know where to look and concentrate the attention – and understand what is being seen. But practice in searching the water in this way and looking into clear streams will enable a separate skill to emerge, almost unnoticed: an ability to see not simply subtle changes in the water or features on the riverbed, but the trout themselves.

After sufficient practice, fish will be found apparently to materialise from nowhere through patches of reflected light, or to become visible through ripples even though the body outline is broken up by the water and dissolved by light.

By the time this stage is reached, the practised angler is able to make casts to specific fish which most others cannot see – or to very localised places on the river, ignoring the rest, in the knowledge that a fish is likely to be present.

By then, the wheel will have turned full circle. Like the trout itself – marvellously honed hunter that it is – the angler will be achieving maximum return for the minimum of apparent effort. Effort there will be, all right: but effort measured in observation and deduction and not in the waftings of an aimless rod.

Lost Fish

There are two kinds of big fish an angler hooks and does not forget, the ones he lands and the ones he does not land. I suspect he dwells longer on the latter. I have not landed many big fish, really big fish, but I have hooked a few. I brood about a couple.

I hooked one on a dapped mayfly on Lough Sheelin, in Ireland. Goodness knows why, soon after dawn and in a flat calm, I should have been fishing the dap, but I was: beginner's inexperience, I suppose. The fly was riding the shot-silk water, close beside the boat, almost under the rod. Then the fly was not there. It was extraordinary. One minute it was there, the next minute it was not there. Then I noticed the leader. It was meandering away, as though being held loosely by the end. I lifted and the rod was wrenched over.

I played that fish for the time it took to smoke two cigarettes – we were all smokers, then – but did not once get it within a hundred yards of the boat. Then the line went slack. The line did not break, it simply went slack and, when I reeled in, there was the bare hook, dangling. I had not glimpsed a mouth when that trout took, seen a turbulence even when it turned and bored down. Yet it had been a great fish, an immense fish. It was a terrible moment.

Later, back in the bar, I told the group I was staying with what had happened. There was an old man in the corner, whom I had seen there before. He had been a ghillie; had rowed Sheelin every working day of his life, season in and season out. He seemed to brood, to speak to no-one, to keep himself to himself and his glass. Then I mentioned the take and I saw him come alive.

When the conversation had moved on and others were holding the floor, he leant over and, as if there were only the two of us in the room, spoke softly, urgently almost. There was an instant, private silence and I heard him clearly through the din. The take, he said, the take, was it... was it... was it as if the fish had taken the fly by the legs, as if the fly had been pulled down by its legs and drowned? Was that the way of it?

Yes, I said, that was exactly the way of it. The take had been that gentle. It had been as if the fly had been pulled down by its legs and drowned. He nodded slowly, studying my eyes. 'Ah, ah yes. That's the way the big fella does it, that's the way he hurts you.' Then he fell silent as though brooding again, as if looking into himself, far back. He nodded every time I saw him, from then on.

Here is a piece about a pike. FROM *The One that Got Away* (1991).

There is a critical point in the life of an angler which comes, if it is to come at all, at the moment he first translates his mind beneath the water's surface.

After that moment, which can come at any time and which came relatively late to me, the rational takes over. He begins to think clinically. Because of the acidity of that lake, fish are unlikely to grow larger than so. Fish of a particular species will certainly not exceed the other. This water will contain whoppers. They will be in the deeps, in the shallows, on the top, near the bottom because, because.

This kind of knowledge makes for absorbing angling. It leads to intellectual and tactical challenges of a thousand kinds and to much thought and experimentation even away from the bankside. But it is a different kind of fishing to that practised before the moment of revelation.

In those earlier, more innocent days, the line does not link the hand and the brain behind it with known possibilities. In the age of innocence, the line is a fine-drawn nerve. Out there it disappears into a twilight deep; here it roots into the imagination behind the bright-wide eyes. It transmits images and excitements and awe, perhaps even a little dread. And so a fish lost in that age when anything might live has no form and no size because clinical thoughts and reason have not yet intervened.

The loss – the effects of loss, the scars the loss creates – go so much deeper in the young. The loss at the age of 12 of a fish of awful proportions is a damaging thing.

The more so, I think, when the fish is a pike. A pike! Clouds gather. Lightning strikes. Rocks split open!

My own leviathan lost was a pike. It is a loss that has marked me for an angling lifetime even though, years later, in a faded cutting about its eventual captor, I was to learn its weight to the ounce.

It was a midsummer's afternoon. The sun burned like a brazier overhead. Bees drowsed. Flowers drooped. Cattle acquiesced beneath shading oaks.

Dace dimpled.

I had made my way upstream from the old stone bridge at Croft, on the Tees near Darlington, spinning for trout and chub with a small quill minnow. My rod was cheap split cane. My reel was an inexpensive fixed-spool. I was in short trousers. Black wellingtons flapped at my knees.

I was prospecting; dropping the quill minnow into every likely place in the weak-tea, North-country water. The bottom was mostly flat ledges of rock and it was to the clefts and steps of the rock that instinct, rather than knowledge, had me aim.

The rod-end flicked, the quill minnow described a shallow arc through the air, there was a muted plop and the bale-arm clicked over. Wind.

And so it went, searching, trying, checking, double-checking. Flick, arch, plop, click, wind. Flick, arch, plop, click, wind.

When I was just opposite the mouth of the River Skerne, where it entered the Tees alongside tables of rock we all knew as 'The Ledges', I saw another ridge on the riverbed.

Flick, arch, plop, click, wind. The minnow landed a little too far downstream. Flick again, arch, plop. Perfect. The minnow went in just above the ridge on the rock and a little to the far side of it. I allowed it to settle for a moment, clicked over the bale-arm, and began to wind again.

But nothing. For the second or third time that afternoon, I had snagged heavily. I lifted the little rod to my right shoulder and pumped carefully. I put the rod to my left shoulder and pumped again. No movement. I moved upstream a few paces and downstream a few paces, trying again. No movement.

I pulled a little harder. The water toyed with the light, reflecting it here, slipping it there. The line played a highly-strung, oriental tune. But still nothing.

Eventually – and it was a serious decision in those far-off days, when everything was funded by an early-morning paper round, when hooks were counted, short lengths of line were knotted and a quill minnow took two days up and down garden paths to buy – eventually, I pointed the rod down the line and began to pull to break.

Something shifted.

I tightened the nut that tightened the clutch slightly and pulled as hard as I dare. And then I saw whatever it was I was snagged into, begin to lift. It was like a drowned log. But no angular arm broke the surface, no cloud of silt drifted downstream.

It is the breaking of the surface that has haunted me. It took long seconds, like some slow, mental dawning. There was a gathering of shades, a convergence of colours, a suggestion of distinctions.

And then the pike's skull was there like an electric shock, paralysing the bright afternoon.

There were the marble eyes, the sprung-trap jaws, the lean, mottled flanks and the far-away, orange, great oars of the tail. I saw all of it, every bit of it, little by little as the fish came up and the water peeled away like ancient time. I was raising the unspoken from my own imagination.

The pike lay on the surface for several moments, as though to convince me it was real. And then it shrugged, turned its head down and swam to the far side of the river. I cannot put it more dramatically than that. There was no effort involved. There was no thrashing of the water. It did not run or dash. It simply swam heavily, irresistibly, to the opposite bank.

Then it swam back. Then it swam to the other side of the river again. Then it returned.

On the seventh crossing of the river, with the fish headed dead away from me, the clutch on the tiny reel jammed, my arm and rod were educated to the horizontal, and the line broke.

Again, there were no dramatics. It did not part with a sound like a pistol shot, it simply broke with a disappointing, low-key switch, as though an elastic band, lightly stretched, had been released. The last visible suggestion of the fish sank away.

I could not believe what had happened. For perhaps a minute or more I stood there, sightlessly staring, held in a kind of emotional death. Then I reeled slowly in and made leadenly to the bank. My companions on 'The Ledges' had seen all of it, could scarcely believe they had seen any of it.

The line was 3lbs breaking strain. The pike weighed 21¼lbs.

Twelve is too soon an age for such a thing to happen.

Fishing for Tigers

The motto of a small club I belong to is, broadly translated, 'there is more to fishing than fish'. Most of us feel that way. Fish are important, of course: there would be no point in fishing if we hoped not to catch fish. But they are secondary. It is the people we fish with, the places the rod takes us, that make our sport what it is. Add to fishing companionship and exotic surroundings and we have a heady mix.

Africa is a heady place: so distant and dark and immense. Its sights and sounds are fit to disjoint the mind, its animals the creatures a child might draw. Africa is so slithered through and prowled through and innocently walked that it is Noah's Ark a continent wide, has the freshness of an Eden, preserved.

To fish in Africa – to fish in Africa on a first wide-eyed visit – is to inhale a kind of opium. FROM *The Sunday Times*, July 8, 1990.

Nothing, nothing at all, had prepared me for it. Not the films, not the travelogues, not the brochures nor the books, not pictures of Sir David Attenborough and his mountain gorillas, not impressions of Dr Livingston being presumed.

We had travelled all morning, eventually skewing and rolling over Lake Kariba's thermals, aiming the tiny aircraft towards the place where the blue of the sky and the blue of the water merged in a distant, hazed limbo. For 30 minutes more we had been in the boat, planing and weaving through the petrified trees that stand in the shallows like great, bleached antlers; had eventually arrived off a low, rocky island where at last we were simply able to sit: heat stilled, rolling gently, fishing.

Then we saw the movement.

We all seemed to notice it at once: Daniel, our African guide from Bumi Hills Lodge; Mick the photographer and me.

Daniel touched the starter button, pointed the nose of the craft towards the island and then cut the engine, its sound and our scent carried away behind us by what breeze there was. We drifted gently forward, hushed over shingle, nosed between rocks. And then soundlessly, surreally, two great elephants, young but weighing tons apiece, appeared on the slope directly above us, not 30 yards away.

Slowly they came, looming until at last the nearest stood massively overhead, silhouetted against the sky: so close that we could hear every rummage and twist of its trunk around shrubs and grasses, hear the effortless uprootings, the engrossed suckings and chewings within the loose-lipped, cavernous mouth.

We had come to Zimbabwe to fish – a kind of alternative safari, I suppose – and at some point we had naturally expected to view big game. But as one of the sights. Probably on some scheduled game drive along well-worn tracks among animals that would look back at us, bored.

Certainly not like this. So immediately, so unexpectedly. So close.

One of the two had a torn edge to one ear; the other had lost an end to one tusk. Both were grey on their lower parts, brown on their backs, shoulder-high plimsoll lines showing they had been wallowing in mud before they swam to the island from the shore.

For perhaps 20 minutes we – the elephants and us – existed in an extraordinary intimacy, a caught-breath silence.

The world slowed. Lizards basked; a snake swam thinly through reflections of clouds; a pied kingfisher dived, picked up a fish and flew off, its victim an indistinct, crystal-dripping blur beneath its beak. And still the elephants rummaged and rooted, lifted and munched, showing no fear of us and offering no threat back.

When, in the fading light I reached for my fly-rod and we pushed the boat out again, Mick rattled off some of the most unlikely photographs any angler can have seen. Then the elephants turned away at last and the magical interlude was over.

We caught nothing in the daylight remaining but, as we returned to the lodge beneath a star-dusted sky, the lights of the commercial boats gleaming like glow-worms from a velvet dusk, we felt no deprivation. The immense, self-contained peace of the two great animals and the sheer sense of privilege in seeing them so close and so free, suffused us both.

We had gone to Zimbabwe because of the talk and the publicity. Zimbabwe was a fisherman's paradise (an overstatement and it didn't matter a jot); we would fish among truly wild animals (we hadn't expected that to be true and it was); we would catch tiger fish, the great predator of Kariba, a fish that leaps like a salmon, fights like a fury and has a mouth like a canteen of cutlery (we did, and it does).

We fished for tigers on Lake Kariba and we fished for them once on the Zambezi River – a privileged outing, that, accompanied by the great Joe Suzman, one of the most successful big game fishermen Africa ever produced. Even though terminally ill and after a bad night and at 80, the indomitable old man was determined that he would take us out himself on his own boat, a little upstream of Victoria Falls.

That was another thin day for fish but again it mattered not at all. The day was all talk and reminiscence and a marvelling at the landscape.

Downstream the distant white plume of spray from the Falls – the Mosi-ao-Tunya, the smoke that thunders – rose 1,000ft into the air. Beneath us the river, a kilometre-wide sheet of grey-blue silk, eased towards its rending and calamitous drop. The shoreline was punctuated with huge mulala palms, their branches and leaves bursting through 360 degrees atop the long, straight trunks – like pale-green fireworks caught in the act of exploding. Hippos grunted in the marshy borders; crickets whirred; the sun burned.

We did get serious about tiger fish, twice: back on Kariba in the Ume River estuary, out from the appropriately-named Tiger Bay Lodge.

I had gone hoping to catch tigers on a fly, but toothy *Hydrocynus vittatus* is interested only in flesh: in particular the flesh of the kapenta, a whitebait-sized strip of silver that supports commercial fleets from both the Zambian and Zimbabwean shores.

I took two on a fly-rod, but only after a little cheating; and we had several more, some of them big, using the carp gear Mick had brought along.

Tigers are handsome fish – beautiful, even, were it not for those carving-knife jaws. They are iridescent silver and blue, their sides striped chain mail, their fins orange-tinged, their deeply-forked tails moving from yellow, through orange to red.

There is one other, special thing about the tiger fish. It has an adipose fin, a tiny, vestigial stump of gristle on its back, just in front of its tail. In the esoteric world where these things are decided, this tiny fin qualifies the tiger fish for classification as something I cannot quite recall, along with the game fish, the lordly salmon and the gentlemanly trout.

Well, game the tiger fish certainly is and lordly, perhaps. But gentlemanly it definitely is not. *Hydrocynus vittatus* is red in tooth and gill and the biggest one I took, a deep eight-pounder, disgorged a shoal of lesser fry into the bottom of the boat.

Tiger Bay produced more than tiger fish, for Mick.

The lodges there offer an extraordinary proximity to the wild. They are made of grass, like so many safari lodge buildings, but at Tiger Bay they are dotted only yards from the water's edge and they have just three sides. There is nothing at all where the fourth wall should be. The open front faces the lake. At night only a mosquito net hangs between the occupant and whatever is out there.

Which is a lot.

The irrepressible Mick, in a mock-macho James Bondian kind of way, declared that he intended to fish through the night while lying in bed, casting through the non-existent wall of his hut. In spite of many cautions against, he felt he could not pass up the chance of fighting a vundu, one of the giant catfish that live in the lake, from such an exotic position.

Fifteen minutes after dark found him hurrying towards the bar stirred, as Bond might have had it, if not shaken.

On his first cast he'd had a grotesque kind of eel; with his second he'd hooked something that had bitten straight through a steel trace; and on the third he'd got a crocodile tangled in his line.

Not all of Zimbabwe's fishing is so creative. There is every day trout fishing to be had in the Eastern Highlands, not far from the Mozambique border.

The road from Harare to Rusape, about half way there, is fine and broad, metalled all the way, at first cutting through farms and plantations, gradually leading to open terrain.

From Rusape to Nyanga, where we were headed, the road becomes a single, narrow metalled strip with the baked red earth on either side, each rare encounter with another car meaning a slight moving-over, two wheels on the strip, two wheels on the earth and a whooshed maelstrom of dust in the air.

We passed the thatched cones of Shona huts just visible above the dry, ripened maize; caught glimpses of village clearings; carried away with us subliminal registerings of old people squatting on the ground, someone stirring a pot, a child with a stick backlit against smoke.

Every few miles we passed Africans sitting in the shade of roadside trees; glimpsed heads as dignified and polished as Benin bronzes; saw cattle being tended by barefoot children, totally alone.

The abiding image, though, as the route straightened and the land fell away to a dry, distant moonscape, was of lone women walking. They were ram-rod straight, had coloured bundles on their heads and often babies on their backs; appearing as though on some dream-like journey from the middle of nothing to the far side of nowhere, travelling a road that stretched away to an infinity that shimmered.

When we reached the highlands we found the rivers, in the main, too steep and fast to fish with a fly. A few streams do have quality trout fishing but permits, incredibly, are difficult to get and it takes a four-wheel drive vehicle to reach the water across country.

Most of the trout fishing is on lakes that could have come straight from Scotland or Ireland: high in the hills, surrounded by fir plantations and outcrops of rock. I fished one of them on a magical evening, drifting along in a tiny boat, facing a sun that was not setting but dropping. It impaled itself on the spike of a fir tree on the bankside opposite, bled red into the water, smudging the clouds. But, in the end, it is not the fishing I remember so much, it is inevitably the African wild.

The two elephants on the island, of course. The three hippos whose bay we tentatively shared (hippos are highly territorial and kill more humans in Zimbabwe than any other animal): a male, a female and a calf swimming towards us – ears, eyes, nostrils out of the water, their tank-like bodies innocently submerged.

There was the crocodile that waddled and slithered disgruntled down the bank when we disturbed it; there were the bullet-eyed buffalo, the fish eagles, the brazen baboons. Especially there were the spring-heeled impala – elegant as ballerinas by day, running in front of the truck at night; their eyes reflecting the torches like moonstones in the blackness, looping and floating disembodied through space.

There was the heat. There were night sounds. There was the smell of earth.

Once again the truth was borne in. The real value of the rod is often not the sport it delivers but the sorcery it performs. Like the diviner's rod it leads directly to water, where so much of the real magic is. And there, like a wand, it parts the curtains that separate the world of man from the hidden, secret places.

It casts spells as well as lines.

Light and the Trout

We do not need to know every last detail of the trout's life to improve our chances of catching fish, but there are some things it is definitely helpful to know. One is the kinds of places fish prefer to live because the consequences of fishing empty water are obvious. Many anglers study entomology because knowing what the trout eats helps them to choose the right fly.

A few go deeper and their interests become more esoteric. I once became intensely interested in refraction and how it influences what fish see and the way fish behave. After a gap of some years I began to think about it again – with some interesting results.

When, many years ago, John Goddard and I decided to write *The Trout and the Fly*, our aim was to place fly fishing in the context of the trout: to consider how the trout sees the world from under water and what the implications of this view might be for the angler.

The book took five years from conception to completion. Those years were, probably for each of us, the nearest we have come to an angling marriage. We shared our thoughts and the work completely. The content of every experiment, picture and paragraph was discussed, debated and argued over – often far into the night. Even though for most of the photographs John had his finger physically on the button, I was hovering just out of shot, manipulating this piece of equipment or prodding that fly into the frame. Even though for most of the time I pushed the pen, John was metaphorically in the room.

As part of the work we studied the way the trout's world physically appeared from below water by sitting under, and taking countless photographs from beneath, a series of large glass tanks which had specially-angled sides. We set cameras into the riverbed. We studied thousands of feet of film shot both above and below water by the BBC's Natural History Unit. We met and corresponded with some of the world's leading figures in the field of fish vision.

We saw all the obvious things that are apparent to anyone with the opportunity to study the surface from beneath. They were the same kinds of things described by several writers who had swum the same waters before us – since Ronalds first raised the issue of refraction and the angler in 1836 and Col E.W. Harding became, in 1931, the first man to our knowledge to study and write for anglers about the mirror, the window, the way different flies appear at various points on the surface, and so on. We agreed with most of the factual observations which these and some other writers had made and written about and we agreed with most, but not all, of the conclusions which these writers had drawn from what they had seen.

There was little point in comparing these various conclusions either with our own results or anyone else's because most of the issues were highly technical and the vast majority of readers would have no possibility of getting under water themselves and so be able to make judgements on the different interpretations offered. We contented ourselves with simply presenting as objectively and clearly as we could, those things we had seen for ourselves; and of setting out our own assessments of the implications.

In some areas, it is true to say, we were able to go further than many others. In particular we looked at the different effects of light on the angler and his equipment and the natural fly at different times of day, including night. With the help of our scientist friends we were able to qualify what we and some others had seen by writing in the context of the known properties of the trout's eye, which has evolved for use under water and so, of course, is very different to our own. We were able to speculate on how the effects of refraction and the known properties of the fish's eye might, when taken together, influence the behaviour of the fish.

Most of what we found or believed appeared in the book's first edition, published in 1980. Afterwards we had only two opportunities to make minor additions. We used the first, in 1981, to add a couple of pages of further thoughts and ideas which came to us after the original text was completed. We used the second, in 1995, to comment on some aspects of the book's contents with the benefit of the experience of the intervening years.

One point that we raised in our additions in 1981 concerned our belief that at least sometimes on rivers, trout on the lookout for food approaching on the surface might lie tilted up towards the surface and at an angle to the main flow. We referred to a picture in our book which seemed to confirm this, to the likely role of refraction in the way such fish might appear, but then left the matter there.

The idea that in rivers trout might not always face the flow head-on was a startling one for many. Indeed, to say that it was startling is an understatement. Several writers expressed incredulity. One correspondent accused us of being drunk when we wrote what we did and drunk when we took the picture to which we referred. The idea flew in the face of common sense and everyday observation. A fish simply had to face the flow. Trout could very often be seen in rivers close to the surface and they were obviously horizontal. If they wanted to watch the surface they simply cocked up their eyes as had always been said. We did not respond, to this or anything else. Time passed. Over the years, John began to follow his separate interests, I began to follow mine.

Much later, I stumbled on evidence which led me to believe that what we had simply speculated briefly is indeed true. It brought me to the firm conclusion that trout do often lie tilted upwards at a steep angle to the flow and the surface, in spite of what appearances and common sense might suggest. What is more I came to this conclusion from quite the opposite direction to the one which John and I originally took. Then we argued *why fish should* lie like this, on the basis of what we knew about refraction and the properties of the trout's eye. Now I believe the case can be made *that they do* lie tilted upwards, on the basis of simple observation. Because the argument leads to some further thoughts that might be of interest, and because these points cannot be taken out of their context, I have set out my thinking in full.

I have watched many hundreds of trout in rivers feeding from the surface. Many anglers have done likewise. There a fish is some distance away, lying close to the surface and apparently parallel to it, just as common sense says it must. Then a fly comes along on the current. The fish tilts upwards a mere degree or two, assumes a narrow angle to the surface, sucks in the fly and then goes back to the horizontal or near-horizontal position with which we are so familiar. I have photographed scores of fish feeding at the surface in this way. So, I dare say, have some others.

One day I was sorting out some transparencies for a talk. For one reason or another I decided to group a series of riseform pictures into two sets – pictures of trout taken from a distance and pictures of trout taken from much closer. On seeing photographs of many trout together, arranged in this way, a couple of things struck me that had not struck me when photographing the fish individually, at different places and different times, over the years.

One was that in the photographs taken from a distance, the fish all appeared to be very thin whereas in the photographs taken from nearer, the fish all looked properly proportioned. More interesting was that while in the photographs taken from a distance the trout were all at that familiar shallow angle to the surface when sipping down flies, the trout near the camera, photographed when close to the bank or from the branches of an overhanging tree, were all at a steep angle to the surface. In other words, although they were doing precisely the same thing in similarly slow, steady flows – lying close to the surface and sipping flies from it – they appeared to be doing so in different ways. There has to be a best way of doing these things. It did not make sense.

Light and the Trout

Of course, I will have known when taking the photographs that the trout at a distance were at a very shallow angle to the surface or nearly so and that the trout close up were at a steep angle because, like many anglers, I have seen it many times: that is just the way trout appear. Even so, the difference caused me to think again, after a gap of several years, about refraction.

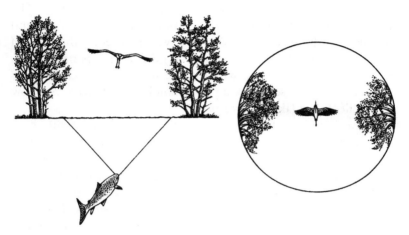

Figure 1. LEFT A side view of the trout's window with some objects in the world above water. *Figure 2.* RIGHT A trout's view of the world above water, with objects near the edge of the window flattened by refraction.

Most fly fishers will be familiar with the principles of the window and the mirror and will have seen attempts in books and magazines to illustrate them. Typically (see Figure 1) there is a sketch which shows at its centre a trout in the water and a horizontal line some distance above it to represent the water's surface. A triangle is shown above the trout by two lines, one either side of the vertical, radiating down from the surface and coming to a point at the fish's eye. The text explains how the angles of these lines from the surface are fixed by refraction and so are constant (actually they are at about 48.5 degrees to the vertical). Because the angles are fixed by refraction and have nothing to do with the fish itself, the triangle above our trout would remain constant and stay with the fish wherever the fish goes and however it swims. Because the angles of the lines are constant, the triangle would get smaller when the fish nears the surface and larger when the fish goes deep.

The triangle, of course, represents a cross-section of the cone of light which comes down to the fish through its circular window. The top of the triangle represents the window. The window allows images of the world above water – trees, birds and the like – to be seen by the fish. The water surface either side of the window is called the mirror. The mirror gets its name from the fact that beyond the window the underside of the water's surface cannot be seen through – it simply reflects what is below it: it reflects the lake or stream bed.

Some books go further. An additional diagram might show the window as the trout sees it from below – as a circle, with some objects in the world outside the water – typically trees – on the edge of the window (see Figure 2). These objects are shown looking much flatter than they really are because light bends most at the window's edge and, in bending, it distorts. The same diagram typically also shows something like a bird in the centre of the window. The bird is not distorted because light bends less the further it moves from the edge of the window towards the centre and, in the dead centre of the window, where it falls vertically, light does not bend at all and so does not distort.

What all such illustrations are showing is how everything the trout sees is governed by the peculiar behaviour of light. In particular they show the way light bends when it moves between air and water and the way that, in bending, it changes the shapes of things.

Now here is the point. It is not only what the trout sees which is subject to the reflection and refraction of light. Everything that we see is also governed by them, most dramatically what we see from the bank when looking into water. We are largely unaware of this because we are so used to it: the world we see is the way our world is.

So now let us forget the trout. Let us think about ourselves.

Imagine standing on the banks of a shallow river or lake in

116

which the water is clear. When we look at the water in the distance, the water shows reflections of trees, sky and the like. We cannot see through the surface in this reflecting area. It is behaving just as the area beyond the trout's window behaves. Let us for the sake of argument, then, call this reflecting part of the surface 'our mirror'.

When we look down at the clear, shallow water close to our feet we can see through it without difficulty. Let us call this place where we can see down into the water, 'our window'. Between the near water through which we can see down to the lake bed and the distant reflecting water, there will be an area where the transition between underwater visibility and overhead reflection, is made. Let us call this general area, 'the edge of our window'.

From the edge of our window we can see down with increasing ease into the water, the nearer to ourselves we look. We get our best view in when looking close to our feet or when peering down over a bridge because there we are looking down vertically into the water – and vertical light does not distort.

Re-enter the photographs. I do not believe that, in spite of appearances, the trout in the distant photographs were behaving differently to the trout in the nearer photographs, when doing precisely the same thing in precisely the same kind of water. I believe they were both behaving in precisely the same way. What was different was my position on the bank in relation to each.

The trout nearer the camera were less affected by refraction because light was bending less between the fish and me – they were nearer the centre of my window and nearer the vertical. Because my view was less affected by refraction, I saw these trout with less distortion. Because they were less distorted, *if they looked as if they were at a steep angle it was because they were at a steep angle.*

The trout I photographed further away were, so to speak, nearer the edge of my 'window' and because they were there the light was bending more sharply between the fish and me. My view of the fish and everything about them, was distorted. They were made to seem thinner than they could possibly be, because the bending light was flattening them in the same way refraction flattens trees and the like on the edge of the trout's window. *And the angle to the surface at which the fish was lying seemed shallow because refraction was flattening that also.*

In other words, the slight angle at which we see a distant trout at the moment it takes a fly is the steep angle at which we see a near trout lying when it is doing likewise. That is point one. Point two is that if a trout that is at a known very steep angle appears to be at only a shallow angle, then a trout at a less steep angle might quite easily appear to be as near to the horizontal as makes no difference.

Of course, I do not conclude from any of this that all trout in all waters in all circumstances will be lying at a steep angle to the flow when they look as horizontal as we are accustomed to seeing them. Some waters are so fast and turbulent that fish cannot feed from the surface at all. Even on those waters where some surface feeding is possible, conditions might not make it possible for a fish to lie comfortably anywhere other than close to the bottom (where the current is slowest), or horizontally facing directly into the flow, with their eyes cocked up as 'common sense' might suggest.

But beyond that I think it is just as John Goddard and I hypothesised years ago. The view is supported by what we know about the trout itself. Scientists say that because of the way light-detecting cells are grouped on its retina, a trout will get its best view of anything when focusing both eyes straight ahead. We know a trout has no neck and so cannot bend its head about as we can. We know that if it has no neck and it wants to get its best view of any object by looking full ahead with both eyes, then it simply has to align its body in the direction in which that object is positioned.

Of course, a trout can get views of lots of things by lying horizontally and tilting its eyes about and most of the time, no doubt, that is how it stays alert to what is happening around it. But it cannot get its best view of any specific object by doing that. It can only get its best view of something it wants to see clearly – say an advancing fly or an area of the mirror where an advancing fly might first be spotted – by facing it fully, with both eyes. And where water conditions allow and the fish is expecting or hoping to see food drifting towards it on the surface, I am now wholly convinced that it lies tilted upwards towards the surface – and that mostly means towards the mirror – when on the lookout (see Figure 3).

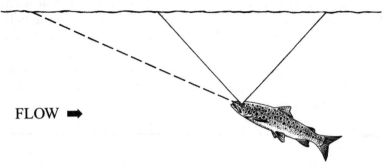

FLOW ➡

Figure 3. The trout lies tilted up towards the surface, in spite of the current, when looking for flies approaching from the mirror.

The angle at which individual fish lie tilted will, I suspect, vary. The angle will be influenced by water clarity, water depth, current speed and perhaps by other factors. However, some general speculation is possible.

It seems likely that the further a fish can see, the shallower the angle of its upwards tilt will be because there must be an advantage in seeing a fly approaching as early as possible – which means as far away in the mirror as possible.

As a fly advances on the current towards the fish so the angle of the fish, if it is interested in the fly, will increase whether or not it has begun its rise to intercept: if the fish wants to keep under close scrutiny a fly that is advancing towards it, while at the same time allowing that fly to come nearer, then it must keep on looking with both eyes from broadly the same place – and so must increase its angle of tilt (see Figure 4).

Then, I believe, a point will come where the fish stops tilting upwards and assumes an angle which remains constant. The deduction is based not only on what we know about the trout's eye but about the way light bends on entering the fish's window.

One thing anyone who has looked up at the surface from below knows is that while a fish often gets its first sight of a fly by the impressions the fly's feet make in the mirror, the fish gets its best view of a fly when that fly arrives at the window's edge: there are certain light effects there that make this view more informative even than the view obtained when the fly is in the window itself. We know from what was said earlier that the angle of the light rays carrying images from the edge of the window down to the fish's eye is fixed by refraction and is constant. The constant angle which the trout assumes on its rise is therefore likely to be that which holds the clearly-seen fly on the edge of the window as the surface is neared.

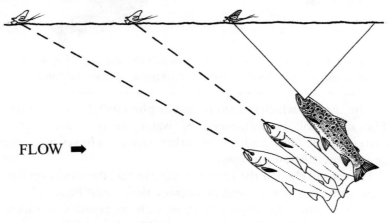

FLOW ➡

Figure 4. The trout increases its angle of tilt to the surface as it concentrates on a fly which the current is bringing nearer. The fish may drift a little downstream and upwards during this process, but the angle of tilt nevertheless increases as shown.

In other words – again as John Goddard and I argued – in the last stages of its rise the trout is likely to be facing up towards the edge of its window at an angle of around 48.5 degrees to the vertical. By holding its body there as it uses the current to carry it upwards and downstream to a point where it can intercept the fly, the fish will retain its best view the whole way (see Figure 5). What is more, because the window is constantly diminishing, the

FLOW ➡

Figure 5. When an advancing fly reaches the edge of its window, the trout positions itself in line with the rays of light coming from the edge and holds itself in this position in the final stages of its rise. Not only does the trout get its best view of any surface fly via these rays, but by holding the fly in them as it rises, the trout puts itself on an automatic path for a perfect interception.

fly will be beside the fish's mouth when the fish reaches the surface. The fly can then be sucked down with all the certainty with which we can lift soup spoons to our mouths and sip.

As a result of all of this it seems that previous speculation that the trout's rise is complex and full of fine adjustments, is unlikely to be true: the trout is guided up to the perfect point of interception as though looking along a laser beam – the straight line of light that marks the edge of its window.

The above all applies to steadily-paced water – and, of course, the fish does not hold itself rigidly, as in the diagrams, which are used to illustrate the principles only.

Significant variations are likely to apply to fish on the lookout for surface fly on turbulent rivers. Here a fish is likely to lie close to the bottom with its eyes either cocked up towards the surface or with its body angled upwards on some distortion in the current. Whichever is the case, I suspect the fish will, once having begun its lift to the surface, instinctively position the fly on the edge of its window as soon as it can, not only to get a better look at what is coming, but to put itself on track for an automatic interception.

Of course, the fish's rise in swift water will not be the same soaring upwards and backwards on the current that the fish in smooth and steady water undertakes: the fast-water fish is likely to see flies late and will often have to drive itself upwards to avoid being pushed far downstream by the current. Even so, inter-ception is likely to be simplified because the fish is likely to hold the fly in the light coming from the lower edge of its window once it gets the fly there in the course of its ascent.

On lakes the most significant variations to the rises described above will be those which take account of the fact that it is the fish and not the water that is moving. Whatever the variation, however, the fish seems likely to angle itself towards the edge of its window in the final moments of a rise from any depth.

Now comes the great admission. It was only having thought through and written the above that I realised how simple experiments could be used to test some, though not all, of the conclusions reached. Like everyone else I had known how a stick appears to bend when pushed into the water. What I belatedly realised was that I could relate the bending of the stick to the concept of my own window and mirror. It is a thought which would have occurred at the outset to anyone with any kind of scientific background, but scientist I am not.

I went to a lake, pushed a stick down into the bed at an angle and walked backwards away from it. In doing so I was careful to keep the stick broadside to my point of view because I wanted it to represent a trout and trout in rivers are broadside when viewed from the bank. The further I went the more the stick appeared to bend and the nearer to the surface that part of the stick below water seemed to draw. So far, so good.

The next thing I did was to wedge a wholly submerged piece of wood horizontal to the lake bed. From directly overhead the wood looked its normal thickness. As I moved away the piece of wood gradually appeared to get thinner – just as the trout in the distant pictures looked thinner than they really were. I fully expected this to happen, but too much had too long been assumed in this entire field: I just had to make sure.

Next, I consciously placed a stick as near as I could to an angle of 48.5 degrees to the vertical (the approximate angle at which light comes from the edge of the window down to the eye of the trout). I then compared what I saw of the stick with what my photographs of trout seemed to show. I steadily backed away from the stick until I was at the same kinds of distances from it as the photographs suggested I must have been from the trout.

From the nearer positions, the apparent angles to the surface of the submerged stick appeared wholly consistent with the angles adopted by the rising trout photographed from close up. From much further away, the submerged part of the stick assumed angles to the surface that were wholly consistent with the angles of the distant rising fish seen in the photographs. While these observations are not conclusive – there has to be room for error either way – the fact that fish at approximately-known distances had adopted a known angle of approximately 48 degrees to the vertical when taking flies, regardless of appearances, does seem to lend credibility to the view that trout lifting to take flies may well hold themselves broadly in line with the light coming from the edges of their windows in the final stages of the ascent.

Finally, I thrust the fully submerged stick into the bed of the lake at an angle of something over 60 degrees to the vertical (the angle of 60 degrees was not critical – I simply wanted an angle somewhere between 48.5 degrees and the horizontal). Then I backed away until the stick was near the edge of my window. Two points emerged. The first was that from a distance the stick appeared as near as makes no difference to be horizontal in the water and had it been a fish, lifting and sliding with the light melting over it, I have no doubt I would have assumed that it was horizontal. The second was that any fish at such an angle to the vertical would obviously be looking deep into its mirror and not, as its horizontal appearance might have suggested, straight ahead into the flow. I think this is clear evidence that between rises a trout may well spend much of its time lying at an angle to the surface – and so to the flow – in spite of what common sense and the evidence of our eyes might suggest.

A Glass-case Trout

Not every fish in a glass case is a monster. Many fish end up in glass cases because they have some other importance for the anglers who caught them. Alas, too often, once marooned in a case on a wall, a memorable trophy becomes unmemorable; an anonymous thing when detached from the experience that made its captor want to keep it.

I once put a trout into a glass case – not an especially big trout, not an especially pretty trout, not even a trout that has ended up being especially well mounted. But anyone seeing it knows why it is there. FROM *Lessons from the Fish* (1996).

It is no longer fashionable to put fish into glass cases – or, at least, it is not as fashionable as it used to be. Most feel, these days, that the best place for a fish is swimming free in the water. Indeed, in some places, now, to kill a coarse fish at all is a hanging offence.

Such Ayatollah-style absolutes are not for me. If I were perch fishing and there were plenty about and I wanted a perch for the pot – perch are excellent to eat – I would not hesitate to take one. Ditto a zander or an eel or for that matter a few gudgeon. But still, in the main, the best place for a fish – and the only place for an inedible fish that is not for some reason a glass-case specimen – is in the water. This is why the great majority of coarse fish we see in glass cases, were caught long ago.

It is different with game fish. Taxidermists do a steady trade in mounting game fish and especially in mounting trout. Given that most trout have been stocked and that all trout on some put-

and-take fisheries anyway have to be killed, there is no reason at all why an angler pleased with a particular fish, should not preserve it.

Personally, I have no problems with the occasional wild trout ending up in a glass case, too.

What I do feel is sad is the way that so many fish in glass cases are reduced to mere furniture. Sometimes the fish hangs there in utter anonymity, with not even its size or captor being recorded. In some instances size and captor are there, in others date and place are noted, too. But nothing more. There is just the glass and some gold leaf and the great fish suspended and lost. A sublime creature has become merely an object, the highlight of some angler's life is reduced to a line of cold gilt.

Yet who has never looked up at some leviathan looking down and not wanted to know more – not just when and where and by whom it was caught, but how? Did this corker come out of the blue or was it a known fish, hunted and stalked? How did it take? What did it take? What was the angler's reaction when he realised he had hooked it? What was the fight like, if that was exceptional? Was there anything other than the fish's size that made its capture stand out? For all that some anglers keep detailed diaries, a diary does not follow a cased fish around. Many a fish in a glass case outlasts its captor and when he goes all that made the creature real, is lost.

I have only put one fish into a glass case and that was a trout. (I did once plan to put a big grayling into a glass case – see A Corker, page 202 – but disaster intervened and put paid to that.) When I caught the trout and decided to have it mounted, I determined to record for good what for me were the essentials: not only the fish's details but the detail of its capture. It was, after all, a story which included one of the most electrifying moments of my fishing career. That moment was as linked to the fish as the fly which seduced it. I wanted to preserve them both.

The fish is on the wall above me, as I write. It is in a bow-fronted case bordered in black and gold. The gold-leaf lettering records the date the fish was caught, the river it came from, the fish's weight and the fact that yes, I really was its captor.

But there is more. Set into the back of the case, as they some-times are, is the fly on which the fish was caught. That is just above the great trout's head. Set into the back of the case just above his tail, is a small card with his story. Not his whole story – there is a limit to how much can tastefully be fitted into the back of a glass case, even the back of a glass case made to hold a river-caught brown trout weighing 5lbs 7oz – but still there is my first sighting of the fish: what it did, what I did and what it did next.

And that moment.

From time to time I reread the story and the whole afternoon comes flooding back. The fish in my case becomes a living thing once more.

It was a hot afternoon in August, 1980. I was on a small river in Hampshire and the water was as clear as gin in a glass. The reach was full of fish, grayling and trout, but on that blazing day there was no hope of a rise.

I had been there before and once, in that place, between the alders and just upstream of the willow that trailed a branch in the water, I had seen a great fish. It was under the far bank where the water was deeper. Even as I saw it, the fish saw me and left. It was quite unhurried. It simply registered that I was there and swam away, part real fish broken by slippages of light, part dark shadow on the stream bed, making upstream. It was heading, when I lost sight of it, towards the old mill and the safety of the deep pool in which, presumably, it lived.

The original sighting of that fish was, that August day, mere memory. I knew that a great fish probably lived in the deep pool some way upstream and that I had once seen it here, in this place; but that was not uppermost in my thoughts: I was simply fishing and aware.

A few yards upstream of the fallen willow branch I saw a small shoal of grayling and a couple of trout. As I watched, deep in cover, they seemed to tense in the water. I cannot say exactly what it was and tense seems an odd word to apply to fish, but it was something like that; a kind of rigid fin-quivering which was followed, almost at once, by a distinct agitation. The grayling slid this way and that, grey as ghosts on the bottom. A trout dropped downstream a yard or two, jack-knifed around in a tight half-circle and faced upstream again, riding a thread of current, sharp-edged.

At first I thought that I had spooked them and froze. A few moments later two other trout came downstream towards me. They stopped abruptly almost opposite, turned to face the current and drifted edgily from side to side. Some of the grayling backed downstream and joined them. No, it couldn't be me. Something was up.

Then he came, close to the far bank, close to the bottom. He was a monstrous fish, the biggest trout I had ever seen in a stream. He seemed to fill up the whole water. He was not hurrying downstream, he was mooching; shrugging towards me in a heavy-shouldered, nonchalant kind of way. He reminded me – his effect on the other fish around him reminded me – of some old-time Hollywood hood. Here comes Mr Big. Look out.

The smaller fish moved aside to make way and then, when he was still a few yards upstream from where I stood crouched and tense, he stopped and turned to face whence he had come.

I had just changed my fly because the willow branches had reached out to acquire the only lightly-weighted shrimp I had in my box. The fly on the leader now was a small, weighted corixa, the next-best thing I had for water of that pace and depth.

I unshipped the fly from the ring it was held on, lengthened a few yards of line and cast. The fly went a few feet upstream of the fish, exactly where intended. As it went in I saw him move forward a little, just far enough forward to make him difficult to see and to take his head into a patch of reflected light.

I thought he probably had the fly. He had to have it, didn't he, moving that way, just then? I hesitated. I wasn't sure. He might not have it. I dared not strike for fear of spooking him in that clear, shallow water and so, trying to tighten gently I lifted the rod a little, instead. It was a tentative enquiry, no more. Too tentative!

What happened next was the kind of transient moment that could so easily have been forgotten, but for the note in the case to remind me. As the rod came up, the line lifted in a drooping diagonal towards the fish. Then it trembled. I saw the line tremble and then felt – I can feel it now – a series of tiny clickings and catchings coming right down the rod, into my feeling hand. It could have been one of a thousand things causing it, but I knew instantly what it was. I have seen the image many times in my mind's eye since: the fish's mouth opening and closing and then opening again to let this strange thing go, the tiny hook tripping and catching through those great, curved, needle-pointed teeth. And then the line fell free. It was an extraordinary split-second. The back of my neck prickled. Goose-bumps came up on my arms. I had fluffed it.

I froze and stared at the place. There was no bow-waving departure for the deep pool above, no black shadow surging under my feet. The fish simply drifted tail-first downstream as though quite unalarmed. He gave a push with his tail in the place he had been before and drifted sideways into the ranunculus.

I decided to wait and watch. I sank slowly to my knees, checked the hook, checked the knot and the leader and then slowly, so slowly, stood half-upright again. Normality returned. The grayling and the trout seemed to relax and settle. Two or three times one of the trout took a passing nymph.

Time passed. Still I did not move. My crouched back and straining neck ached. I kept lifting first one foot and then another to ease their stiffness. And then, without ado, the great fish came out again. He simply drifted sideways from the ranunculus into open water.

I was ready. I already had the nymph in my left hand and enough fly-line out through the top-ring to flex the rod the moment I began to move it. I cast at once. The nymph went in perfectly, a couple of yards above him and exactly on his line. 'He didn't have to move', the note in my glass case reminds me, 'I saw the white of his mouth as it opened, as though he were stifling a yawn. Again I tightened and the rod went savagely down. This time he was on!'

I didn't record the rest. I remember some of it vaguely – the bulldozing run upstream towards the deep pool, a desperate attempt to get into the tangle of the fallen willow-branch, much splashing, quite a lot of mud, water in my wellies. But already the detail of that is fading because, presumably, it was not unusual enough to be worth preserving.

Yet all the memorable things are there. The fish, of course, to look at again and again: that small head; those huge hook-tripping, neck-prickling, goose-bump-raising teeth; the massive shoulders and back; the oddly small tail. His details and mine. The fly he took. The story of the events that led to his downfall.

In the great scheme of things my fish is no leviathan, I know that well; important though he is to me. But I would like to think that where he goes, that realisation goes, too. The realisation of just how much has been lost from those ancient glass cases; how the great fish of centuries have been reduced to mere objects and how the triumph felt by their captors has been lost for good.

If only some commentary had been mounted beside them, forgotten moments of history might be thrilling us now.

Advances in Fly Tying

The artificial flies which most of us use today have evolved over hundreds and maybe thousands of years. They are extraordinarily effective, as every trout and salmon ever caught on one will testify. Now the room for manoeuvre and truly significant advance seems limited. We have, in the main, to be content with tiny advances – one of the reasons why, year in and season out, this or that trivial adjustment to an established fly or tying style is being pushed by someone, somewhere, as his claim on immortality.

Of course, the fact that there seem so few places to go does not stop us travelling. We always have as a spur the example of the director of the Patents Office who, 100 years ago, is said to have resigned because there were no more major inventions left to be made. This piece is about fly dressing developments in recent years; and about the way, too often, we are seeking the unreal. FROM *The Salmon and Trout Association Yearbook,* 1993.

T here can be no angler who has not experienced it. He catches a fish. There is someone down the bank who sees the splash and the commotion. There is a pause – it is not too long and not too short – and then the stranger's rod goes down and his shadow looms up. There is some sidling interest in this or that and then another pause.

'Er, what did you get it on, then?'

Even those who write about fishing occasionally bank something and over the years this is a pantomime that I have been a party to, many dozens of times. Among all these occasions the essential supplementaries have been asked only occasionally: not simply 'Er, what did you get it on?' but 'How did you fish it – and why?'

The difference between the two approaches is immense. The first seeks some magic fly, the second recognises that it does not exist: that for any fly to have any magic it must be placed where the fish can see it and fished in some stimulating way. In other words, that fly and fieldcraft, tying and technique, cannot be separated.

And yet still – human beings being human beings – the search for the magic fly goes on. Still fingers fly and patterns multiply; still claims for this space-age tinsel or that feather from a duck's bum or the other bit of wool from Aunt Nellie's cardie, escalate. This pattern is a killer, that is a corker, the other is essential and will not fail. And all the while anyone with fingers to count can see that if even a fraction of these flies were truly to be needed, any fly box designed to contain them would need wheels at each corner and an engine behind.

Looking back over the last few years, it has to be said that the most important development in fly tying is not any in-dividual dressing among the thousands produced or even any given style. The most significant development is the increasing size and number of fly-fishing magazines and the ever-increas-ing acreage that is devoted to the fly tyer's vice.

The progression has been inevitable and relentless. More magazines and pages have meant more columns to fill. More columns to fill have meant more writers at work. More writers at work has meant an ever-more competitive scramble to make an individual impact on the public mind and on the affections of the editor who calls the tune.

In the need for circulation and stimulation it is the man who can ring the changes and pull the surprises, who gets the space and the reputation. And so, at the centre of the fly tying centrifuge, the world turns faster and faster and more dressings whirl off into the available space. There is nothing wrong with any of this. That is the way that the real world is. But it does mean we have a lot more flies to consider.

It is not a cycle that has been applied to salmon fishing. There have been few fads or serious developments in salmon flies, for a long time. The hairwing fly has whiskers on, the tube and the rest are old hat. Something ephemeral and black will, in skilled hands, catch most fish that are going to be caught, if it is in the right size and at the right depth and travelling at the right speed.

On the dry fly scene, there have likewise been few developments.

In our book *The Trout and the Fly*, John Goddard and I, among other things, showed how the surface fly looks from below the water and, as an exercise in fly tying realism, we sought to reproduce these optical effects in a range of somewhat complex dressings.

These dressings have largely floated by on the stream of time: not because they are not effective, or even because they fail to offer something worth further development, but probably because they are fiddly to tie and commercially uneconomic.

Other stabs at looking at the dry fly anew have also come and gone without being taken up on any commercial scale – again no doubt partly for the reason given above and partly because the traditional style is so effective as it stands.

Dry fly fishing as a tactic has moved on a little, especially on stillwaters.

The increasing attention to the dry fly on lakes is an interesting development that has coincided with the warmest years of the century. The resulting increase in water temperature may well have had an effect – as yet unquantified – on the natural history of insects and on the behaviour of fish, increasing the amount of surface fly and extending the time in which the trout finds the surface layers of the water congenial.

So the weather may be a contributory reason for more fish now being taken from the top. Another reason has to be that some exceptional anglers saw an opportunity, experimented successfully and then wrote about their results. More space for the dry fly in stillwater magazines equalled more awareness among stillwater anglers, equalled more stillwater dry fly effort, equalled more fish: in other words, the old cycle busily turning again. We have seen hopper dressings for fishing on the surface, emergent ephemerid and dun dressings for fishing in the surface, suspender dressings for hanging from the surface.

Of the three, the last two are the most significant. The style of the last type, the suspender dressings, are not, incidentally, the original brainchild of either John Goddard or myself or, indeed, any other British angler, as I often see written. Credit for the principle on which all suspender patterns are based – a nymph hanging suspended from the surface film by a ball of buoyant material – belongs entirely to the brilliant American angler Charles Brooks, who worked on the style in the early 1970s.

It is a long way from the delicate confections fished at the surface, to the lake bed. A very long way. It is a journey that brings us into Dog Nobbler territory.

If there has been a single dressing style that has marked – scarred, some would say – the last few years on stillwaters, it has been the Dog Nobbler. The principles on which this style of dressing is based likewise are not new: indeed, the jig fly principle, which is what it is, was around in the US for many years before it was picked up and brought here.

The Dog Nobbler is essentially a hook with a cannonball pinched behind the eye at one end and a marabou tail that waggles about, at the other. It is enormously successful, especially when retrieved in little bursts and pauses that cause the fly to dart and dive and dart and dive, always with the tail waggling behind, suggesting life.

It is not a form of fishing that appeals to me, but it has caught vast numbers of fish for many who otherwise might have gone home blank. To that extent the Dog Nobbler and its kind serve a useful purpose, devalued only when success with such dressings inhibits people from developing further.

What else? Well, there is the Booby. The Booby is a dressing that looks like the extra fly in the box when a Dog Nobbler and a suspender pattern have been left together, overnight. It is a fly with a bulbous, buoyant head – typically two balls of polystyrene – and a wobbly, marabou tail. It is fished along the bottom from a sunken line, on the end of a short leader. It can be tied as a lure or to suggest an insect – say a damsel fly.

But, again, it is the technique of which it is an integral part that is interesting: a technique which enables it to be inched and pulled and wobbled close to the bottom, for a long way, through deep-feeding trout. Even this is not new. The principle of fishing a buoyant lure on a short leader on a sunken line close to the bottom was written about by several writers, from the late 1960s onwards.

Anything left? Not a lot. So rather depressing? Not at all.

The factors which drive fly tying forward – indeed, the factors that drive the sport forward as a whole – are the unpredictable and sometimes perverse behaviour of fish on the one hand and the need for anglers grappling with the problems posed, to give expression to their individuality and creativity, on the other.

From time to time, these two will lead to an advance of a kind: but always it seems destined to be an inch forward rather than a yard; and always it will be the fly in the context of an approach and not some dressing that is magic of itself.

The Wrong Time

In a properly ordered world there would be a place and a time for everything and everything would happen where it should, when it should, on cue. Angling is not a properly ordered world. It would be difficult to think of any activity less ordered. Lady Luck smiles one day and not the next; sometimes on this person, sometimes on that. There are some folk on whom she never seems to smile at all. Even when the siren appears at her most benign, she can deceive.
FROM *The Times*, October 7, 1994.

He was staring out into the middle of the lake focussing, at a guess, on nowhere. He had all the regulation gear: two carbon fibre rods trained like ray-guns over the water; two regulation rod-rests, each armed with an electronic bite alarm and LCDs and buzzers that would let him know if a fish thought about breathing on his bait.

He had two whizz-bang reels. He had bags of commercially-formulated, pre-packaged bait. Of course, he had a 'bivvy', the small, omnipresent tent that carp anglers set up regardless of the time of year or the time of day or the weather: a product which, like so much else in carp fishing gadgetry, symbolises the triumph of marketing skill over angling need.

He was half-kneeling next to a mountain bike that lay on its side, one elbow on his raised knee, chin resting in his cupped hand. He was a fresh, clean-cut lad. About 12 or 13, I guess, plus the lifetime he had aged that day.

I had been on the other side of the lake when I heard about him: not fishing, simply walking quietly by the water; listening, looking, dissolving my own thoughts in the dissolved clouds in the flat-calm surface; absorbing it all and being absorbed.

I had been talking to an old man who, for all his not inconsiderable weight was standing two feet off the ground. After several decades of trying he had just taken a monstrous carp. It was the kind of carp that is spoken about softly when incense is burning. It had been a corpulent carp and it had steamed off like a befob-watched alderman, cannily knowledgeable about the lie of the local land, certain and unstoppable when up and running. But he had landed it.

The seasoned old man had done what any carp angler would do on the capture of such a fish. He had photographed it, admired it for a lingering moment and set it free. And then he had begun to recount the story of its capture to the starstruck throng that had emerged from the bushes and the bivvies all about. When I arrived he was, quite properly, sparing them no detail; waxing lyrical over the biggest fish he had caught in a 45-year career: a fish nearer 30lbs than 20lbs.

Then the news came that the young lad on the far bank had also had a fish. The older man seemed not to notice and continued with his saga. His audience was absorbed and stayed. After a respectful delay I dropped back from the edge of the group and sought out the boy.

Yes, he said, he had just had a beauty. It was the first carp he had ever had and he had taken it first-time out. I popped him the question. 'Twenty-one pounds. Twenty-one on my Dad's scales!'

He was pleased but not, it seemed to me, overly so. Accepting is probably the term: accepting, but no more. And then he gazed out over his rods again, trying to concentrate but clearly miles away, thinking no doubt of his great fish returned and perhaps the size of the next fish to come.

In one way, of course, I was delighted. Who would not be delighted for anyone who has caught a 21lb carp? But it was not an unqualified delight because the young lad clearly did not know how big a 21lb carp is. He did not realise that it is a fishing career long, a young man's ambition wide, many an old man's disappointment deep: the kind of fish a thousand anglers pursue but never see, much less ever catch. Even today a 21-pounder is a fabulous fish.

There are, of course, some who would not see it so. Carp fishing in recent years has been assailed by a technological madness and a psychological disease. Only numbers matter: numbers defining the ever-more unnecessary specifications of tackle; numbers of fish caught and avoirdupois. Twenty-pounders are caught regularly from some waters, often enough the same fish over and again. Thirty-pounders are taken some-where, most weeks; forty-pounders are taken most seasons. Among the medallion men and the jaded palates, a twenty-pounder is an also-ran. But in the real world it is a glass-case specimen, though people don't put their fish in glass cases much any more.

And therein lies the problem for the young lad now. In a properly ordered world, every angler's 'best fish' would get steadily bigger with the passage of time. Ideally, some difficult but achievable milestone would eventually be reached; but only rather late in life, after much effort and anticipation, when the pleasure and significance of it could be appreciated fully.

Certainly there would be no pole-vaulting leap that would take the roach angler from 12 ounces to 3lbs or the chub angler from 2lbs to 6lbs or, for that matter, the man I know who is pursuing the gudgeon record from three-and-a-half-ounces weighed and witnessed, to four ounces, no kidding.

Certainly – because it would be too cruel – there would be no move for a carp fisher from nothing to 21lbs, just like that.

The carp that the old man caught at nearer 30lbs than 20lbs was a carp properly caught at the proper time and the pleasure it gave lifted all who saw him. The 21-pounder caught by the nice young boy staring out over the water at nothing in particular, was not such a fish. It was the wrong fish in the wrong place at the wrong time: and it had been caught by someone of quite the wrong age.

It may well have left the lad, for all his equipment, with every-thing a young angler needs but hope.

A Pike and a Trout

We live in one of the most artificial landscapes in the world. Our country is so crowded, our need to feed and house ourselves so great, that there can scarcely be a square inch of ground on which we have not imposed our will. By day things happen as we decree they should happen. But not by night. When darkness falls and the curtains are drawn, the wild world returns: the bright eyes peer, the ears prick, the victim's short squeal cuts the air.

In water, by day and by night, our reach is more limited. Even on the truly expensive rivers, rivers that are managed for trout as intensively as the land is managed for livestock and crops, life below the surface is not easily controlled, no matter how orderly things might seem. Under the weedbeds and in the deep, dark holes, nature rules as she has always ruled. FROM *The Times*, November 30, 1994.

T here can be no more cloistered and artificial world than that of the English chalk stream. For decades and in some cases for centuries the banks of these lush waters have been sculpted and manicured as habitats for trout.

Weeds are cut to channel the flow so that silt is carried away and clear lies are created. Branches are trimmed to ease access and casting. In some places the bankside grasses are mown low as lawns. Mink are controlled, coarse fish are netted and transferred elsewhere. Always pike are kept down.

And yet for all this latter-day artifice, nature rules life in these waters, still. She showed how completely late one afternoon.

I was wading up a short piece of stream that I am sometimes

invited to fish. It is at the end of the club's otherwise well-tended water and it is left overgrown for those who like the challenge of the tricky fishing that such places afford. Because it is overgrown and difficult to fish with a fly, few members bother to fish this place and, relieved of the angling pressure, the few trout there can grow large.

I had reached a narrow place where there was a willow behind me and where an alder grew over a dark pool opposite. Shrubs grew densely all about. I was looking near the alder, hard under the bank where fingers of tired comfrey trailed, when I saw a movement.

It was a fish, of course. I did not see it but the way the water heaved and rolled was unmistakable. A few minutes later I saw the movement again. It was a faint, semaphore wink followed at once by a distortion of the reflections as disturbed water welled up.

The pulse of light came again and began to move. I stood still and watched. Another pulse and a disturbance of the reflections; another pulse and a soft welling-up. It was a fish all right, a trout. Its white belly was facing me broadside to the current. It seemed in two parts, the tail faintly flexing and catching the light, the head and gills at that time still. And as the questions formed and my puzzlement deepened, I saw the pike. It had the trout across the middle, fast in its jaws. The pike was about 4lbs, the trout about 1lb.

For a while the two fish lay in a place where a shaft of light slanted through the trees and I could see them clearly. I could see, as well, that something was wrong.

When a pike takes another fish it normally grips it broadside in the middle of its jaws, impaling it on the huge, canine teeth in the lower jaw and pressing it against the densely-packed, inwardly-sloping teeth of the upper: the fine-as-needles teeth that all point the dreadful way down. The grip seems to paralyse the victim which, after some moments or minutes, is turned to face head-in towards the pike's throat; and the pike suddenly gulps it down over the curving teeth that allow easy entry but no way back.

This pike had the trout broadside not across the middle of its jaws but seemingly far to the back where the two jaws hinged; and the trout seemed trapped but not mortally-stricken. The trout would lie still for a while and then tremble or fret; or it would bend slowly, tense as an iron bar; or it would twist violently up and down. Sometimes the trout's movements were so strong that I could see the pike's head being physically wrenched. Several times while I watched the pike swimming slowly, the struggles of the trout seemed to turn its captor off-course.

It was a while before I realised not only that the trout could not move but that the pike could not move it. The trout must in some way have been caught awkwardly too far back in the larger fish's jaws, perhaps out of reach of the largest teeth in the lower jaw and clicked onto the little teeth in the upper. The trout that had been the intended victim was gagging and choking the pike that had taken it.

I watched the two fish, fascinated, for over half an hour: the pike now high in the water and now low, now clearly visible, now faint. Time after time the pike would lie still and jerk its jaws as though confirming what I guessed: as though trying to move the trout, without effect.

At one point I saw a second trout that I had not noticed before, quivering in the water as though at the horror of it all; and then it whirled around in a wild circle and dashed away. Gradually the movements of the pike seemed to weaken and I saw the white of its own belly as it wobbled. The fish's jaws jerked and gagged, the trout struggled and remained fast.

When the two fish disappeared into the deep pool at the base of the alder I waded across and looked down from the bank. I found the pike lying over a mound of silt that had collected behind the tree's tangled roots. Even as I watched, the trout somehow fretted and twisted again and the pike's head was dragged and worried sideways and down. Black clouds bloomed and I lost sight of them; then bloomed and thinned and bloomed blackly once more. The silt mound heaved and smoked for a while. Eventually it settled. I saw neither fish again.

When eventually I looked up from that terrible place I saw an opal sky and a kingfisher's blur. Two swans were feeding sedately only yards away, melting their necks little by little as they reached down for the bright weed that grew there.

I walked back towards the car through the peace of near-sunset, with the manicured valley spread about. I walked past the trees that had been neatly trimmed, over grass that had been recently mown. The keeper, who was adding some refinement to a piece of bank, called goodnight and I replied.

And I left behind the world where the old laws prevail, for all the frivolous tinkering that we do.

Casting to Trout
on Rivers

Casting a fly to a trout is not a difficult business. Casting a fly to a trout on a river, effectively and consistently, can be a different matter. Now it is not only the mechanics of the cast that need to be accommodated but the movement of the fish in the water and the effect of the current on the fish, the line and the fly. It is surprising how many anglers never come to grips with these problems – the first especially. FROM *The Times*, September 30, 1994.

I quite often fish rivers with anglers who cast repeatedly to rising trout and who fail to bring up the fish. Nothing unusual in this, one might think. Is it not, after all, the demands of the sport and the perversity of trout that gives fly fishing its glorious appeal?

Indeed so. What makes matters noteworthy is that, for all my companions' ability to drop a fly onto a riseform, they have seemed completely unaware that they were not covering the fish itself. It is an observation several have been able to prove to their own satisfaction when I suggested they cast to slightly different places and up each fish then popped like a good'un.

There are several small wrinkles to casting for rising trout that can greatly improve the chances of success. Not the least of them lies in understanding what happens when a fish in a river lifts to the surface. A trout that is taking flies from the surface lies beneath it in a comfortable place and looks upstream and upwards for signs of an approaching victim. When it sees a fly getting near, the fish does not dash vertically to the top. Most often, it simply adjusts its fins, gives a necessary impetus with its tail and allows the current to do the rest. But as the fish soars upwards on the current, so the current is also carrying it downstream.

The result is that the point where the fish intercepts the fly – and at which the riseform is seen – is downstream of the point where the fish has its lie and the place to which it will immediately return. The deeper the fish and the faster the water, the more pronounced the downstream drift will be. Quite often a fish will be looking for food a yard or yards upstream of the place where the rise is seen and where the unaware angler casts.

The first wrinkle, therefore, is that any cast on a river to a surface-feeding fish should be to a point upstream of the riseform and not to the place where the rings first occur. Exactly how far upstream is a matter of experience and observation: but most casts made to the ring of the rise will be behind a fish that is actually moving away. Small wonder, then, that a rise does not follow. No fish can take a fly that it has not seen.

There are other wrinkles worth storing away concerning drag.

The most difficult cast to any fish is the one to a trout lying in slow water on the far side of fast water. The problem is familiar: the instant the fly alights in front of the fish, the fast water snatches the middle of the line and pushes it downstream in a belly curve. Then the fly on the end of the leader attached to the line drags away from the trout, often in a way that alarms the fish.

There are many wondrous leaders on the market that are designed to assist a 'perfect' delivery of the fly: usually one that the advertiser defines as a clean unfurling of the leader so that it goes down, pencil-straight. Casts like this look very pretty, but they are worse than useless on rivers and the products that insist on delivering them should be avoided. The last thing a river angler wants is a straight delivery of the leader, not least because most of the time drag – which may or may not be visible to him – will set in at once, even on slow water. Casts on rivers –

especially rivers with tortuous, drag-inducing surfaces – should be designed to put wriggles and loops and upstream curves in the leader. The aim is to achieve the maximum of natural drift for the fly before the push of the current straightens everything out and drag sets in.

Of course, one has to be sensible about this. There are some situations in which the difference of the speeds in the water between the angler and the trout are so great that no loops or wriggles or curves will do the job. There are also circumstances in which the wind or some other feature makes any kind of controlled cast impossible. But, given practice and half a chance, such casts can be achieved often enough to make the difference.

Loops and wriggles can be formed by throwing the line high and letting the leader collapse higgledy-piggledy on the water. Upstream curves can be achieved by casting with the rod held horizontally instead of vertically and by checking delivery of the unfurling line at the last moment. The line will more or less straighten, but the leader will curve sharply around.

Another way of defeating drag is to choose carefully the point from which the cast is made. Very often, the best place will not be the traditional one diagonally downstream from the fish. Indeed, this position is often the worst.

Any cast to a mid-river fish from a downstream point on or near the bank means that the cast is cutting diagonally across the current and giving the water the maximum amount of line to play with. The result, again, is often instant or early drag.

Most often, the best place to cast from will be a point directly behind the fish. Trout cannot see a low object – like a crouching or wading angler – directly behind them and the line from such a position does not go across the current but into it. From here the downstream drift of the line and the fly will be at a more even pace. The next best casting point is often opposite the fish. The minimum amount of line is made hostage to the water and the wriggle and curve casts can be made to greatest effect.

The net result of these very simple ploys is more fish seeing the fly and a few extra inches of drag-free drift towards them. Oh yes, and more rises as well.

Fishing at Night

There was a time when I would fish in all kinds of weather. As a lad, rain and tempest could not keep me from the water and earthquakes and hurricanes would not have uprooted me, once there.

Things have changed. I have been soaked to the skin and been chilled to the bone enough. I will still go out in bad weather if the inducement is great enough, or if I have an arrangement with someone; but beyond that, if I can choose, I opt for fresh green spring and balmy summer. The longer I fish, the less intense I become; the older I get, the softer I want it.

One day, in a tackle shop, I met a man whose special love, he said, was to fish from a beach, through the night. In winter. Especially, he said, in winter. What manner of man was this, I mused? What kind of folk were these who, while the rest of us are abed, will opt for the spray and the knife-edged wind? I decided to go and see.

Eight forty-five, the beach, Hayling Island, Hampshire. It is one of the coldest nights of the year.

The light from the Tilley lamp defines the world: here picking out detail in the shells and stones with a scalpel sharpness; there touching the dark timber breakwaters that partition the beach on either side; in front marking the slow, arching waves and the rolling white cordage of surf.

There is an odd sense of intimacy within the confines of the light; a cosiness, almost, that defies the bitter air. There is no awareness at all of the world immediately behind us: of the garish corona of the empty amusement arcade; of the silhouetted houses and flats; of the cars that drive along the coast road above with steam wisping and curling from invisible exhausts.

The light-cocoon of the Tilley lamp, the rolling and hushing of the waves, insulate completely.

The two men tackle up with practised efficiency. There are rods, reels, boxes and buckets, all distributed neatly beneath the high shingle bank. Whole fish and chopped fish, half-enough for a market stall, are laid out for bait in newspaper packages. Ragworms freshly dug from the beach, stir in the sand which keeps them separate and dry in the bottom of a tub.

Trevor bends a small, plastic capsule in his fingers and the chemicals inside it mix and glow brightly. He attaches the capsule to the tip of his rod.

Paul, a few yards away, is ready to cast. He walks towards the waves holding his rod high, controlling the erratic pendulum of lead and the large piece of mackerel that swings contrarily beneath it.

Side on to the waves he looks briefly left towards the winking lights of the Solent, then turns and addresses his rod, now pointing inland and low. There is a moment of stillness – a weightlifter's kind of stillness – then smoothly and easily, he swings. The rod describes an arc from the flats just behind us to the lights of Bembridge on the Isle of Wight. The weight and the bait yaw out into the blackness, then he sets the rod in its rest and watches.

It is an action that is being repeated over and over along this one strip of shingle; a ritual that is repeated night after night by thousands of others elsewhere. On the blackest and wildest of nights an invisible army is out there while the rest of us sleep. The wind howls, the waves crash, the cold seers but still the light-cocoon of the Tilley lamp beckons.

There are probably as many motivations for being in such a place in the dead of night in the dead of winter, as there are people who do it. The man with the dog a little way down the beach has no doubt what attracts him.

'The peace and quiet. This is the one place in the world where

I can get away. I've got three kids and a wife in a two-bedroomed house. I work in a factory all day bending little pieces of metal. The noise is terrible and the boss is on my back. Out here I'm away from everything. The dog comes too. We'll be here till high tide, tonight.'

High tide is at one o'clock in the morning. By 10.15pm the peace and quiet of the man with the dog have not been disturbed by anything. Nor has his rod.

'The fish are not important, anyway. I just think it's beautiful out here.' He uses the word without any trace of self-conscious-ness. It is no more than a statement of fact.

At a few minutes to eleven, a hundred or so yards further on, a man called Mick is landing a pouting. It is about eight inches long and, as he reels in, the fish spirals upwards into the brilliant beam of the lamp that he has on his head. It is a beautiful, mother-of-pearl fish with eyes that are bright, black pools.

When the fish is about shoulder high, Mick stops winding. The pouting hangs motionless for a moment and then begins to revolve slowly, as though for inspection. Globules of pure light drip down from its tail.

Mick has a different reason for being here.

He drops the fish back into the surf, to go free. 'That was a pout, but it could have been a cod or a bass or anything. A really big fish. I've had all my big fish at night and I'm always expect-ing to get hold of a monster. Maybe it's something to do with the dark, I don't know. So I'm relaxed but I'm tense, both at the same time. I've been coming since I was a kid.'

'So have I. Great, this.' Mick's friend has just recast after landing a pouting of his own. He settles himself onto a large tackle box and speaks without turning. His chilled breath drifts up into his own head light, floating and curling, defining the beam with a passing precision.

Mick and his friend know the shoreline and the seabed well; they know the routes the fish follow as well as any salmon man knows his river; they know all the likely hot spots as well as my trout friends know their lakes. Even in the darkness they are casting to specific places that experience and reconnaissance at low water have taught them. They cast from specific points on the beach, in exact directions, marked by the position of known lights. But it is slow going. 'It's been terrible lately, bad as I can ever remember.' It is Mick speaking. 'Used to be really good, this section.'

It is already midnight. Back on top of the shingle bank I can still count 20-odd lamps. It is a completely separate, self-contained community of self-contained units, each of them encapsulated in its bright dome of light, each of them with its wigwam of rods, propped umbrellas, arranged boxes and occa-sionally-moving figures. Huge shadows reach along the beach and rear up into the sky whenever someone close to a lamp moves between it and me.

A distant clock chimes. One hour to high tide. A police car drives slowly by and I am studied in a casual way. Bembridge has put out the lights.

At half past midnight, near the end of the line, someone has a stove going. No sooner has the man tending it poured himself something into a mug than the receptacle is dropped and the stove goes flying. The dark figure dives for his rod and picks it up, feeling for a second take that doesn't come.

By the time I reach him he is examining the hook. It has been stripped clean.

'Channel whiting, that's what that was. Typical Channel whiting bite. Bang-bang, then nothing. They've got hundreds of tiny teeth all around their mouths. Incredible how they can strip a bait like that, without getting hooked. They do it all the time.'

The stove is righted and some soup from the pot is salvaged.

'No, it isn't a typical night down here. Usually there's more action than this. But things are definitely getting worse.' Shades of my salmon friends, shades of wild trout.

There is a clatter of shingle on the bank behind us and a figure half-slides, half-lopes down it. By 1.30am my companion Dave has been joined by three others. Dave scrapes the last of the soup from the bottom of the pot. One of the recent arrivals lights a second cigarette. Serious fishing, along this part of the beach at least, has stopped.

It has been a painfully bad night, but still the conversation is good-humoured and low-keyed. There are exchanges of repartee quick as ping-pong rallies, discussions of technique, debates about the future of fishing, recollections of fishes past, tall stories.

At 2.30am I make ready to leave.

'Coming back tomorrow?' Dave asks the question, pausing as he pumps up his lamp. 'Oh, a pity, that. There's going to be a real blow-up. Could see some real action tomorrow, couldn't we, lads?'

It is a curiously distant voice that, moments later, follows me from the light into the engulfing dark. 'Well, you know where to find us if you change your mind.'

Even after a bitterly cold night in the dead of winter and with scarcely a fish to show, optimism reigns. The light-cocoon of the Tilley lamp, the rolling and hushing of waves, insulate completely.

Whales and Trout

Whales are not fish, though they lead fish-like lives. Because they are mammals and breathe air, they need to surface frequently so that they can blow and inhale. To be beside a whale when it surfaces and blows, is not easily imagined.

I was once asked to go to Newfoundland to write about humpback whales. The piece which resulted was largely about my first awesome experience of seeing a whale, close up. To describe the surfacing and the dive of one whale in detail seemed a useful way of conveying something about whales in general and why these gentle and intelligent animals have so seized the public mind.

A few days after the article was published, I had a letter from a trout angler. The writer said that the whale was the ultimate fish. To have its emergence and dive described in such detail, from such close quarters, had from that point on enabled him in his mind's eye almost to become a fish. It had magnified by proximity and size a life that had always been otherwise distant and unreal no matter how hard he looked or what books he read.

What the whale did was what the trout did, he said, writ large. He felt he could now swim with the trout, ride the fish's back while it was head-and-tailing. He drew a parallel between whales and men and the trout and small flies.

I will quote something from the first piece because of that interesting reaction, which might strike a chord among others. I will quote it also because it sets the background to a second, originally unplanned article which followed – about trout.

First, that encounter with a humpback whale, on a small boat, in the open sea. FROM *The Sunday Times*, June 6, 1993.

The air is still. The sun is low on the distant cliffs and fingers of light splay out. Only the boat moves on a softly breathing sea; the boat and the gulls, tinsel-flickering across the hazed blue sky. A gentle, rhythmic pat and lap of water measures out the silence.

'Blow. 7 o'clock. One thousand.' The clipped voice, the precise, minimalist directions come from Peter Beamish, the scientist who owns the craft we are on. He is standing high on the seat behind the wheel, bronzed and bearded like some latter-day Ahab.

Fourteen heads – English, Canadian, American, German – turn; 14 pairs of eyes search the water beneath the dark-grey cliffs, pick out the ostrich-plume of spray that stands on the air. Beamish slips the engines into gear and opens the throttle. The big screws bite. Ceres settles back on her haunches, then leaps forward like an untethered hound.

The half-mile or so takes moments, all whining engines and rummaging air. The low swell hits the bottom of the boat with the sound of flailing chains. Spray hurtles past the gunwales like chopped ice. And then the engines are slowed and closed off. The bow settles and again we wait.

Close by, between us and the cliffs, a huge, circular, slightly convex dish of water widens. Kittiwakes and terns circle and cry, straighten and launch themselves into it.

'That's where she dived. She'll show in about another two minutes, probably around 11 o'clock.' Beamish again. He knows that humpback whales typically dive for around seven minutes and surface for two. This whale has been down for around five minutes, already.

'Humpback. 12 o'clock. Forty metres. Wait for the blow.' I hear the blow close up. It is like the cut-short burst of steam from a vast locomotive.

Even then I am not prepared. Before leaving home I had debated with myself, rationalised, scaled down. Forty feet long? Fifty feet? That's twice from here to there, nearly as long as that, a bit longer than the other. But in the sea she won't seem so big. In the vastness of the sea she'll be in perspective.

In the sea, in the vastness of the sea, lifting, lifting, metre by metre, the whales goes on and on, filling up the consciousness, blacking out the sky.

'Oh!' 'Ah!' 'Look at her!' 'Isn't she huge!' 'Isn't she beautiful!' 'Isn't she . . . isn't she . . .' But someone's words won't come. The voices are excited at first, then awed; take on that altered pitch reserved for talk in cathedrals. Cameras whir and wind, lenses zoom, shutters click.

Beamish slips the boat into gear again and takes us nearer. We move right in behind her and keep pace, easing along at around five knots.

I am in the bow and can see right down the centre of the whale's back, her black sides glistening, curving out smooth and round. She looks as big as an upturned ship. I can hear the water sluicing along her flanks, see the vortices building up behind her head, watch them turn and purl along the thin line of her wake.

Though she could swamp us with a careless roll, smash us with a blow of her flukes, there is no sense of danger. She is benignly accepting, curiously calming. She makes no move to accelerate or turn down or lose us. She may well be studying us, in return.

'See the arms? See the arms? The arms are right below us!' The flippers of a humpback whale can grow to 18ft long and in the North Atlantic they are usually white. I can see one gleaming luminously to my right and then, with a start, see the other out to the left. *Megaptera* – big wings – is appropriately named.

I crane over the bow and look down. It is as though we are riding her. The arms are planing out to either side and there, right beneath me, are the flukes of the tail, undulating. It is a leisurely, graceful movement, though massively powered, as though by a turbine.

'She's going to dive. She's going to dive. Wait for the tail.'

Our two minutes are up. The whale eases a little to our left, seems to quicken a little, to gather herself into herself, and then her back arches slowly, the water spilling and sliding off it in glistening curtains, the spine arching and gleaming, the roundness of each great vertebra picked out in scallops of light.

'Get ready with the cameras.'

Then one of the most memorable sights on earth: the tail, the insignia of a conservation movement, the image from a thousand dazzling posters, lifts.

It unfurls from the surface in endless slow motion, the immense flat flukes cascading water and light, the irregular, barnacled edge only metres away.

For a moment it seems to pause, to wait as though for the appreciation of the cameras; then it straightens and the underside shows. White markings, unique to every individual, are visible for a moment; and then the tail slowly slides down, melting little by little at the base. The sea rushes in, briefly foaming; the phosphorescent arms plane downwards, luminously fading; the trail of bubbles behind her dissolves to nothing; and she is gone.

Here, now, is the second piece which emerged from that trip. It was written directly to anglers and resulted from conversations with some other visitors who, unconnected with me, happened to be whalewatching from the same place, at the same time – and to be anglers themselves. It is simply the way different newspapers schedule different kinds of articles that led to the first piece appearing so long after the second. FROM *The Times*, September 30, 1992.

Watching whales move and feed off Newfoundland not long ago was a life-enhancing experience for all aboard the small, fast craft we used. For the anglers among us, there was a special fascination as we watched these marvellous creatures recreate on an unimaginable scale, the kind of behaviour a trout displays when moving and feeding back home.

To link the behaviour of whales with the behaviour of trout may seem a bizarre thing to do, even for an angler, yet it is only the scale of events that is truly different.

Time after time it was possible for the anglers on board to see before the non-anglers, fast-moving minke whales head-and-tailing through the surface at a distance. The fleeting dark appearances, the cross-hatched patterns their movements made in the low waves, attracted the eye in just the same way as the movements of head-and-tailing trout feeding on a lake. The size of the creatures matched the openness of the sea and from a distance the overall impression was much the same.

While crossing open sea in which no whales had been sighted, it proved possible several times to spot where whales had surfaced earlier because of the large patches of calm water that they had left behind. In diving down they had produced huge, upwelling convections of current that had risen and flattened out the waves.

This flattened area of water – the 'footprint' – that a diving whale leaves is precisely the same kind of clue that a trout offers when it is feeding below the surface, on ascending nymphs.

Because some nymphs move quickly or awkwardly, the trout have to move quickly to grab them. As the fish move, so they displace water; and the faster they move the more violently the water is shifted. Where violent movement occurs near the surface, the result will often be an upwelling of water that will flatten out the ripple directly overhead. The appearance of such a round, stunned area of water in the middle of an otherwise consistent ripple pattern is where an experienced angler will cast his fly, when the beginner has noticed nothing.

Using the same principles it was possible, in favourable conditions, to follow the progress of some whales when they were below the surface. Such was the power of their flukes that even when many feet down, each beat sent turbulence welling upwards to the surface. A line of such turbulence showed the route the whale was taking.

In trout fishing, the passage of a fish below the surface can sometimes also be tracked because of the tiny movement of the water's surface that the swimming fish makes: a movement that can distort otherwise clean reflections or create winks of light in areas of dark water, or winks of darkness in patches of light.

The signs of a whale feeding on fish would be familiar to anyone who has seen big trout savaging fry.

Before trout attack, their presence is often betrayed by an

agitation among the prey and some small fish will leap clean into the air in panic. When the big fish do attack, all gaping jaws and flaring gills, the water often erupts as the intended prey hurl themselves everywhere in desperation.

In an area where whales are feeding, even when none can be seen, the next likely place for an upward lunge will sometimes be indicated by fish leaping from the sea in just the same way.

The gulls off Newfoundland took the whale-trout parallel even further. They behaved exactly as would their cousins on Rutland and Chew. Both trout and whales, in the violence of their feeding, stun and cripple small fish that they do not eat. Then the birds move in, circling and gliding before diving down to pick up an easy meal.

By watching the gulls in Newfoundland we could often gain some clue to the whereabouts of distant whales. By watching the birds on British lakes and lochs, an observant angler can often gain clues to the whereabouts of distant trout – or of localised insect hatches, which will attract them.

There were even parallels for the angler who stalks individual trout in clear waters.

Any experienced stalker knows that the last thing he should expect to see is the clear outline of a fish. What he recognises first is something that appears inconsistent or foreign in the area of water into which he is looking.

There may be a suggestion of sepia in an area of darkness that on scrutiny becomes a fish's tail. There may be a pulse of light as the sun catches the side of a turning fish, or even a pinprick of white when a trout opens its mouth to suck in a nymph. It is such hints and winks and suggestions of fish, that the stalking angler looks for.

And so it proved with the whales albeit, again, on a different scale. Many times we found we could see humpback whales below us or near us, when our non-fishing companions could see nothing.

In the north Atlantic – though, curiously, not in the south – the huge flippers of the humpback whale are white. In the clear, clean, plankton-laden sea these flippers glow with a phosphores-

cent light; and they often reveal the position of a whale long
before it has surfaced or after it has dived. Even in a low wave we
found that provided the sun was up, a whale could be located
because of the intermittent, semaphore pulse sent out by its
arms.

There was, it is obvious, no magic in any of this: it was simply
a case of knowing the kinds of clues that swimming fish offer –
and then of recognising them when produced by the whales. It
was absorbing enough for experienced anglers. It would have
been an education for a beginner struggling with the small clues
at home.

Trout from a Cake Box

Oliver Kite, somewhat unkindly, once said of stillwater trout fishing that it was a case of 'chuck it out, pull it back and when you can't you've got one'. Well, stillwater trout fishing can be like that. So can all fishing – including fishing on Kite's own chalk streams if we do not know what we are doing. Reaching that wondrous stage where we know even a little about what we are doing and are trying to achieve, can take years by the water.

There are some kinds of practical experience we can obtain away from the water. There is one step we can take that will carry us a mile. My own average catch increased several hundredfold, one year to the next, because of it. Yet I know scarcely anyone who has given it a try. Here is how. From *The Times*, April 10, 1992.

My friend Lefty Kreh, the famous American angler and casting instructor, tells a wonderful story about a demonstration that he once gave.

With a single movement of his rod he drove an entire fly-line to its full extent, out onto the grass in front of him. The crowds of spectators to either side, gasped.

With a single backcast, he then lifted all of the line in front of him, out in a straight line onto the grass behind. Another gasp.

He rolled the line to the left and he rolled the line to the right. He executed steeple casts, Z-casts and trick casts of a dozen kinds. Gasp followed gasp followed gasp. Finally, Lefty removed the butt-piece of his rod completely and proceeded to repeat the entire performance using the top half alone. Stunned silence.

'Okay', said Lefty after this mesmerising display. 'Anyone got any questions?'

A pause, then a man in the crowd stepped forward. 'Tell us', he said in a coaxing stage whisper, 'where did you get the magic rod?'

The story preserves a great piece of humour; and yet it conveys a truth that will be recognised by anyone who writes about fishing, or teaches it, or is perceived in any way at all to be successful at it. By far the most common question that comes through the mail or is asked on the bankside is the one that seeks the short-cut; that tries to winkle out some imagined piece of magic; that asks the dressing of the 'secret' fly.

There are very few short-cuts in fly fishing, but there is one. It is a short-cut that will save years of mere hopeful presence at the waterside; that will teach a great deal about flies and the ways they might be fished; and that will provide anyone with a serious interest in improving his fishing, with many hours of added fascination without even leaving home.

It is to make a small aquarium, to stock it not with fish but with aquatic insects and to watch how they behave. It is 21 years since I write that I made my own such aquarium; and it is 20 years since, by applying what I learned, I saw my catch from lakes increase, season on season, by around 600 per cent.

There is no magic involved in the process and no special knowledge is required. Running water is not necessary because insects that live in still water are in the main very similar to those that live in running water. Almost any kind of receptacle can be used and, for what it is worth, my own 'aquarium' was a clear plastic cake box about 12 inches square and five inches deep, that I filched from a kitchen cupboard.

I simply went along to a nearby gravel pit, placed some sand and silt from its bed into the bottom of the box, put a large stone in the centre to create an island; and then slowly filled the box to within half an inch of its lip, with water from the same place.

While the contents were settling, I trawled along the bottom of the lake and among the weeds with my daughter's minnow net and dumped anything from it that moved, into a jam jar. I then sorted out a few of all the various life forms I found I had and placed these into the aquarium. A couple of sprigs of oxygenating weed from a pet shop to keep the water vital, a separate bottle of water to top up the aquarium as the water in it evaporated and the job was done.

Anyone prepared to invest the same tiny amount of effort now will reap dividends within minutes. They will also introduce themselves to a form of entertainment so dramatic and absorbing that television will lose its bleary charms and hot food will congeal on the plate.

The first few trawls of the net will produce many of the insects that lake trout eat – and on which so many artificial flies are modelled. They will also dispel any unquiet thoughts that lakes might be filled with wriggly horrors and show aquatic insects – unlike many of their land-based brethren – to be fascinating and often beautiful creatures.

The most likely insects to be found are olive nymphs, damsel fly nymphs, corixae, freshwater shrimps, alder larvae and sedge larvae complete with cases of sand and meticulously cut leaves; midge larvae and pupae; and freshwater snails which, for all their lack of charisma, will creep slowly around the inner surfaces of the glass, keeping them clean and algae-free.

The mere act of lifting the minnow net from the water will add flesh and meaning to the Latin names so often unnecessarily used in angling books – and will clarify much in their sometimes confusing texts. It will show how awful are most of the imitations sold in the shops. Studying these creatures as they bustle about their daily lives only inches away from the end of the nose, will give the clearest insight into how they move and hatch and die – and so how artificial flies should be moved and fished on the end of the line.

For those who tie their own flies, the aquarium provides nature's own models for copying; and for those who do not, it will provide the basis for making far more discriminating choices when artificials are being bought.

The aquarium will give other things, as well. The metamorphosis of the darting olive nymph into the diaphanous and elegant winged fly, the hatching of the midge pupa into the often beautifully-coloured adult, the struggles of the corixa as it darts to the water's surface, acquires a bubble of air and then labours mightily to carry it to the bottom to breathe, will absorb and fascinate, give even a sense of privilege and wonder.

More practically, the aquarium will give a new sense of confidence when rummaging through the box and fishing a fly, especially when the trout are rising and so are known to be feeding. It will bring an end to the desperation of lucky dip and 'what did you get it on?' and 'is it true they want something green, today?'

Over all, a profound sense of satisfaction will emerge not only from the fact that fish are being caught, but from a knowledge of why they are being caught.

This, without doubt, is the greatest benefit of all. It is at this point, and not with any dazzling rod or 'secret' fly, that the real thrill of fly fishing begins.

The Red Float
Incident

There is something about a float that makes a statement about angling: that refines to a fine, visible point all its wonder and suspense. The porcupine quill pinning reflections to a lake, the bob float gliding and pirouetting its way down an eddy, carry a freight of emotions.

Coarse fishing is less dependent on floats than it used to be. At one time floats were all that most people – and certainly, most lads – used. Today, technology holds the ground. As split cane has given way to glass and carbon fibre and the centrepin has been overrun by the fixed spool, so complex rigs and electric alarms have carried all before them. The porcupine quill is stuck in the ark, the bob float has almost bobbed out of sight.

I am unfussed by this. When I go on my ritual coarse fishing trips once or twice each year, I let progress whirl right on by. I try to use a float whatever the conditions because I love to watch one. I choose it in a time-honoured, low-tech way. These days, floats are less a means of catching fish than of recapturing wonder. FROM *The Guardian*, July 13, 1985.

Blankety-blank years ago a small, tubular Bakelite float, brown on the underside and red on top, pirouetted its way down a sunlit reach of the River Tees, curtsied in an eddy and plopped down out of sight.

A home-made bamboo rod, the rings held on with elastoplast, the reel made from a bobbin and some part of a sewing machine, was jerked awkwardly skywards and in that sun-shot, far-away instant one three-ounce gudgeon and one small boy were hooked.

The fish, as first fish inevitably are, was taken home, paraded and cleaned, then pomp-and-circumstance fried in the pan; I found a sport that has materially influenced my life.

Since that time, I have always loved floats. But then, all fisher-men love floats for the reason just illustrated. Most anglers begin fishing when they are young and, because children cannot handle complex equipment and need something to hold their attention, they often begin fishing with floats which are both simple to handle and absorbing to watch.

And so, think of a float, conjure a childhood. Remember innocence and light and school holidays and bicycle rides and bright red 'Oxo' tins packed with sandwiches and excitements and first experiences of a thousand kinds.

Remember fish. I have memories, scarcely formed, of long-handled nets and minnows from the Tees and, somewhere, a suggestion of something vastly bigger that my sisters and I trapped between two nets and left head-down in a jam jar one night and found belly-up the next morning.

There was the gudgeon, of course. There was the 13-ounce dace – a dace I have never bettered – from the still water above Broken Scar Dam. There were the chub that all one long summer dashed out from the roots near green-sleeved Blackwell to grab the gleaming blobs of cheese I floated past them.

There were the 13 barbel in an evening from the Swale at Ainderby Steeple and the night I filled a keepnet so full at the same place that I had to empty it out once before continuing to fish. There were the trout, vibrant and highly-strung, that I took on a legered minnow during a school summer camp.

There was the litter on the table through the long winter evenings and the kitchen booby-trapped with tackle and trip-wired with line. Hooks spilled, shot rolled, soil stirred in hidden containers. There were floats – old floats, new floats, partly-made floats – everywhere. Forgiving parents high-stepped and side-stepped through it all.

Remember hypnotism, too. Few physical things in my life have had the same mesmeric effect as a float, have proved as visually riveting, as bobbingly electrifying, as that magical object waltzing and gliding down a fast-moving stream, dipping to the bite of a fish, maybe this time a monster.

I use floats less often, now, indeed go coarse fishing less than I used. But I have a lifetime's collection to choose from when I do. I have long floats, short floats, thin floats, fat floats. I have bungs big enough to moor your boat to for pike and minute, hardly-there-at-all floats for dace and roach. I have antennae floats for fishing in the wind, slider floats for plumbing the depths, transparent floats made to look like bubbles. I've got floats designed to dip to a bite, rise to a bite, lean over to a bite; floats made from cork and quill and pith and wood; floats designed to catch more fishermen than fish (and jolly successful they've been at it, too).

And yet when I reach for one now, take one of those annual trips on the time machine, my choice is rarely based on technical criteria. I can get technical about trout. Very technical. But I don't want to get technical about floats. My attitudes are based on nostalgia and idiosyncrasy, like the relationship some have with their hats. I tend to use just three.

The most important float of all, my Bakelite, road-to-Damascus gudgeon float won't be there, of course. I lost that when I was about 12, hoofing it from a bailiff on the posh Darlington Anglers' water on the other side of the bridge, where ordinary lads weren't allowed: marvellous, sleeking chub water that oiled under alders and curled around a bend.

But the other Big Three will be there: the 'red float incident' float, the Swale barbel bagger and the Irish pond waltzer, a gigantic quill that I used in Ireland for bream and tench; marvellous, special-memory floats more vividly described by the experiences which left them their names, than by technical specification.

There's no room here to go into the stories of all three. Maybe some other time. But I will mention one, the red float incident.

It evokes exactly the romance that all floats conjure.

It was a baking summer's day on a pond I'd stumbled on somewhere, in some woods. The red float had sat motionless, for hours, the short white porcupine quill through its centre skewering its reflection to the surface. The sounds of bees drowsed on the air; the flowers and sedges hung heavily over the water; my rod drooped in its rest, exhausted.

And it was hot. My word, it was hot. I watched the float, hypnotised. The world closed in. The float changed shape, distorted, blurred, resolved and twisted.

Time passed. The whole day could have been a dream. I could have been a figment of my own imagination. And then the float slowly began to go down.

I watched it disappearing, the water blurring its shape, water and light welling up and glinting around the cork, over the quill, the whole form of it gradually getting fainter in detached slow motion.

After what must have been an age the spell finally snapped and I was fused and alert, my hand hovering over the rod-butt as though it were a six-gun, my eyes zooming in on the water, wide awake. And there sat the float, motionless as before, still cloning itself in the surface.

I could hear my heart still thumping inside, but the sense of relief was enormous. I hadn't missed one, I hadn't missed one. Any bite is important to a small boy. But on that dark, still pool, that Cyclops' eye deep in that wood, who knows what might have been? Who knows what awesome shades passed what ponderous, aldermanic lives beneath its weeds – and sometimes fed? I settled back again and relaxed.

And then, long moments later, through some slow permeation, something caught my eye: a faint wink of light, and then another; the faintest dying, ebbing rings, several yards across. Rings that had my motionless float, dead-centre.

I grabbed the rod in a mixture of panic and dread and struck as hard as I could. There was nothing, absolutely nothing. No fish, no bait and to my total disbelief, no hook either. The line had been bitten clean through, inches above the hook.

And that's it. No dramatics. Once again, no searing accounts of my fight with great fishes. Simply one small boy on a high summer's pond, experiencing a surrealist moment that he has remembered all his life.

Of course, from time to time, logic threatens to intervene. Given the size of the pond, the kinds of fishes it probably held, the modest sizes probably achieved because of this and the other... but when all that stuff creeps in, I push it out again. Who can know – really know, I mean – what might have been in that deep dark pool that sun-stilled day? Or what might have happened if I'd been more alert and struck when the float first sank?

Like I said, that's the marvellous thing about floats: think of a float, magic a memory, conjure a childhood. I do it all the time.

Richard Walker

'It has taken some 15 million years from the time when man first stood upright, for him to evolve into what he is today. For all of that time, except for the last 10,000 years or so, his survival was totally dependent on his hunting ability, and in the case of some races, it still is. Man developed, but he still needed to preserve the instinct to hunt – without it he would have become extinct. That instinct, so essential for survival for millions of years, has not been lost in the few years during which it has not been strictly necessary; thus fishing is a way of fulfilling a basic need.'

The words come from the preface to the 1975 edition of *Stillwater Angling*, Richard Walker's most famous book. They are not only the clearest explanation of why the need to fish goes so deep in some men but a clear defence of angling in the face of subtle shifts in modern public opinion.

Walker had no difficulty in resolving the worlds of ancient man and modern man. Indeed, he rejoiced in both. He felt the early fish-hunger inside and brought to bear on it not only an exceptional brain and steely determination but specific interests in natural history, genetics, science, technology and (as it happens) palaeoanthropology. His achievements in coarse fishing especially were so many, his influence so deep and pervasive, that even in his own life-time he was seen by many intelligent and informed anglers as being probably the most important identifiable figure in the history of the sport so far. These men recognised not only what Walker was doing, but the implications of what he was doing. *Stillwater Angling*, for those men then and for many others now, might just as well have been called *The New Testament of Angling*. Richard Stuart Walker was

166

born in, appropriately, Fishponds Road, in Hitchin, Hertfordshire, on May 29th, 1918. He died in Biggleswade, Bedfordshire, on August 2nd, 1985. He arrived on stage in a dramatic way.

It is unusual to be able to fix any important development in angling precisely in time. It is the more unusual that a profound moment in angling history can be pinpointed almost to the minute. Yet that is the case. The time was shortly before 5am on September 13th, 1952. It was then, after some hours of inactivity on Redmire Pool, in Herefordshire, that a length of line was drawn out from between two metal contacts and in the dead of a coal-black night, a buzzer sounded.

Richard Walker recalled later, what happened next. 'I raised the back of my hand under the rod to feel if line was being taken and felt it creep slowly over the hairs ... I struck hard and far back ... I encountered a solid but living resistance.'

The common carp Walker had hooked weighted 44lbs – a fish of such massive size and interest that it was given its own name and was to spend the next two decades in the aquarium at London Zoo. Clarissa broke the existing carp record by an Irishman's mile.

The significance of such a catch today, when so many carp are artificially fed to great size and the pressure of some carp fishing amounts to a form of abuse, is difficult to convey. Until then big carp had about them an almost mystical air. They were the uncatchable fish. Few people tried. Walker and the small group of intimates he led, tried and often succeeded, most famously at Redmire. There is no doubt that Walker would have come to national prominence anyway; but that one great fish brought him to attention at once.

Nobody would argue, of course, that Izaak Walton is not more famous than Richard Walker and that Walton's pastoral hymn *The Compleat Angler* has not outsold the books Walker wrote by probably several hundred to one. But Walton's book was a work of literature and social revelation, not intellectual angling force. No-one went fishing in a different way because of what Walton wrote, though they may well have appreciated milk-maids and cowslipped banks the more.

Nobody would argue, either, that there have not in the past been able writers who made practical contributions. Francis Francis and Cholmondeley Pennell were among the all-rounders. John Bickerdycke and J.W. Martin were among the coarse anglers. Halford and Skues were among the trout men. Hugh Falkus was an outstanding figure among Walker's contemporaries and a man who dominated salmon and sea trout fishing like no man in his own time before him. But none of the coarse men was remotely as influential as Walker either in what they contributed or the numbers they influenced, and for all the brilliance of the game anglers, each of them was dealing with single – or in Falkus' case two – aspects of game fishing alone. Walker's principal influence was on coarse fishing, the biggest branch of angling of all. He changed the mindset of millions.

Walker had been writing long before the capture of his big carp. He used a nom-de-plume, Water Rail. The year after his carp he was asked to write a weekly column in the new *Angling Times*. It was a labour he kept up almost until the last. He used this column and his books and his other articles and his talks and his correspondence which, at times, took on the aspect of a blizzard, as a platform for his views and as a conduit for information.

Walker was interested in all fish and in every legitimate means of catching them. Above all he was interested in the challenge presented by big fish. His attitude was clear. He believed that no fish, no matter how large or difficult, was uncatchable provided it was fished for with sufficient determination, in the right way, in the right place, at the right time, with tackle capable of hooking and landing it.

Of course, in saying that one has said quite a lot. But it was an attitude he both preached and practised. It was what gave him Clarissa.

Walker had long before determined to catch big carp and had caught many. But he wanted a leviathan. He set about it, as he set about all other angling problems, with relentless logic and undiminishing zeal. First, he learned as much as he could about the species, acquiring a freight of knowledge about the fish that no angler before him had remotely possessed. Then he found a lake known to hold leviathans. Then he studied the fish in that lake to the point where he could identify individuals. Then he laid siege to them.

So single-minded was he in the year he took his record fish that he caught only four others from Redmire Pool in 460 hours' fishing; which is to say that he fished four unbroken days and four unbroken nights, for each single bite.

When he was alerted to Clarissa's take it was because he had developed the world's first electric bite alarm, at a stroke putting the night-fisher's bobbin of dough and fold of silver paper and the torch trained on them both, into the ark. When he over-powered the fish after a memorable battle it was because he had designed – Walker was a brilliant mathematician and engineer – a rod to tapers of his own calculation, to do it. He had even hand-built the split-cane that he made the rod from. Up to that point, no rod had existed that would have helped to put such a fish on the line and handle it so effectively – and every carp rod today is based on the precepts he laid down. When he lifted the fish from the water it was enmeshed in a net of – again – Walker's own design and manufacture.

Walker brought many of his ideas together in the first of his books, *Stillwater Angling*, which came out the following year. It was an epoch-making work. It set out clearly, for the first time, how great fish of different species could be caught not by luck but by skill, science and the will to catch them. *Stillwater Angling* preserves the essentials of all that Walker subsequently wrote about coarse fishing and, in its discussion of lakes, provided much that is of value to trout fishers also.

The place where he subsequently wrote most was in *Angling Times*. His column was a remarkable thing. Over time – one piece a week, every week, for 33 years – his column contained all that *Stillwater Angling* contained, constantly updated. That, though, was not its great significance. His column's great significance was that the paper in which it appeared reached millions of ordinary anglers across two generations, mostly anglers who would never have bought and read an angling book in their lives. *Stillwater Angling* reached the book buyers. His column reached the rest. It reached the man on the lakeside and the riverbank. Little by little, week by week, it laid out the essentials of scientific coarse fishing in language anyone could understand. Year by year, decade by decade, angling on the lakeside and riverbank changed because of it. So did tackle. So did pretty well everything else.

Walker picked away at every nook and cranny of coarse fishing as though with a scalpel. When each nook and cranny was picked clean, he shone a searchlight into it. He wrote with authority of the natural history of fishes, of fish behaviour, of entomology, of the refraction of light, of stillwater stratification, of the effects of wind on water temperature and the effects of oxygen (and lack of it) on fish. He wrote on hooks and rods and reels and baits and barometric pressure. He wrote on landing nets and night lamps and luminous floats; on vision and vibration, genetics and growth, tactic and strategy. On what makes a good packed lunch.

Much of what Walker covered had been written about before, though not always in an angling context. His genius was to draw together everything that was relevant; to distil and refine it; and to lay it all out in the context of a total approach to the water.

Of course, it was all backed by personal achievement. Walker was about nothing if he was not about results. He not only caught the record carp but numerous other large fish of many species because he set out to catch them – large barbel, roach, rudd, chub, dace, pike, bream and perch among them.

There were, in addition, the game fish. Walker had the reputation in trout fishing of being a coarse angler but he was the most accomplished of all-rounders. He caught wild brown trout from the age of seven, on flies of his own tying. He subsequently caught very large brown trout and immense rainbow trout, including a 'record' rainbow that had been reared and stocked in a small stillwater fishery – though predictably he did not claim that gong.

In later life Walker began to devote significant time to the challenges posed by the growth of stillwater trout fishing in lakes like Grafham and Rutland and to write about them in the game fishing magazines. Some of the old hands writing at the time and who knew nothing of his background, or felt it was not relevant, or who simply resented his directness and formidable self-belief, were incensed as though by an upstart. It caused not a few established trout writers, destabilised by his knowledge and logic, to attempt to dismiss him – attempts which were not only ludicrous and futile given the manifest sense of what he was saying, but which were to diminish these writers' own reputations in the process.

Trout anglers have much for which to thank Walker. Amid all else he seized on carbon fibre when it first appeared and designed the first fly rod in the world to be made of that material – and he created a veritable hatch of new artificial flies and lures. It helps to illustrate the thinking Walker brought to stillwater trout fishing – the contrast between his approach and the conventional approach – by touching on just one of these dressings.

One evening, after a day's pike fishing with Fred Buller and Ken Sutton – Buller the pike master and Sutton the angling administrator – I drove with Fred to Dick's house to have dinner with Dick and his wife, Pat. Over the meal I said that Dick should send a set of his own dressings, tied by his own hand, to the Flyfishers' Club in London. The club's premises are the nearest thing Britain has to a fly fishing museum and Pat was descended from one of the club's Victorian founders. Dick sent the flies, but somehow they went missing. A couple of years later and only a few days before he died I asked our mutual friend Pat Russell, whom I knew was to visit Dick, to ask for replacements. Dick went through his own fly box and the dressings he picked out now hang framed on the club's walls. Of course, they are all exquisitely tied. One of them – Walker delighted in such names – is a Dambuster.

The Dambuster has two big, stiff cock hackles on it. They are separately wound, one at the head and the other down the shank. It has a dark, peacock-herl body. It has a fluorescent, arc chrome tag. A ludicrous design, one might imagine, looking at it.

171

Well, perhaps – except that the fly was created to catch fish feeding within inches of dam walls, on the bugs that are washed off them from both above and below the surface, by incoming waves. The stiff hackles enabled Walker to cast the fly right onto the face of the dam from a drifting boat, without damaging the hook on delivery – and to pull the fly slowly off the stones, into the water, without the hook point snagging or picking up debris. The fluorescent tag was designed to make the fly easy to see in the turbulence of the waves. The dark body was sufficiently bug-like to appear as food once a trout had been attracted by the tag.

Bingo.

Throughout his life Dick Walker kept a schoolmasterly order in the angling press: rapping knuckles, patting heads, putting the wellie in. It was an order which, after his death, disappeared. Many writers began making claims that few in the general reader-ships could challenge on the basis of knowledge. Most among the few who could challenge, would not be bothered. Walker had the knowledge, the inclination and the energy to challenge always, at every turn: not only other writers but 'fact', folklore and received wisdoms that did not stand the test of his own experience, observation, and formidable powers of reasoning.

Dick Walker had a significant though not enormous impact on trout fishing and a great influence on tackle design. Indeed he designed a range of products big enough to stock a tackle shop's back room. But those who see him as the most important known angler of this century and likely to prove the most influential in the sport so far (let those with another candidate stand up and name him) are considering none of this.

Here is the reason they believe as they do. It is because Walker caused vast numbers of anglers of all kinds – though mostly coarse anglers – to think to an extent that no generation of anglers before them had thought. While his debt to his friends should not be forgotten – his thinking was stimulated and qualified by a group which included Peter Thomas, Fred Buller, Fred J. Taylor and Maurice Ingham – it was Walker who, by his own efforts, drew angling out from the dark ages: who brought science and logic to a sport that up to his appearance had largely been lost in myth and adrift on potion.

In his lifetime, Dick Walker gave two generations of coarse anglers a clear sense of purpose for every fishing action. In doing so, through them, he wrenched around the tiller for generations to come.

Planning the Trout Season Ahead

I never did meet an angler who lied. I never did meet an angler who said he felt tempted to exaggerate, even by a teeny bit, the size of any fish caught or the skills needed to seduce it. The very word 'fisherman', one might think, would make a ringing definition of truth. Yet here we are, regarded by society at large as folk who would turn truth into elastic and facts into bendy toys.

We are not being helped, I have to say, by a growing trend within our own ranks. It is the way some anglers, while not openly refuting the claims of others, have at times been calling specific details into question. I have even noticed my own friends beginning to raise eyebrows when I now report – as I naturally do very often – yet another astonishing feat achieved in their absence.

One year I took it all to heart. I became so frustrated by their nitpicking that, to forestall the feigned amazement which would certainly have resulted otherwise, I published a whole season's results in advance: not only what fish I was going to get but where and how and – the killer, this – how huge they all would be. I found it helpful. Other great performers might like to spike their own friends' guns. Here is my own plan, for guidance. FROM *The Flyfishers' Journal* (Winter Edition, 1982).

These Doubting Thomases get everywhere. Fred Buller, who's seen enough of big pike to know better, had great difficulty in accepting that I once caught a 78-pounder on a Blue-Winged Olive. Buller said that all the big pike he'd taken on the dry fly had been preoccupied with caenis and seemed unable to understand why any large pike might feed on anything else.

It was enough – and I say it frankly – to make me wish I'd kept the fish to show him and not returned it to the water at all.

My friend Pat Russell had a similar problem when we were out for a day's coarse fishing with the fly. In the only 30 minutes in the day that we were out of direct sight of one another – we were cut off, as ill luck would have it, by a bend in the river – I took a grayling of 9lbs 2oz and a brace of roach that went 6lbs apiece.

Russell used the fact that I'd returned all these fish to the water before what he called 'witnesses' could be found, to question my seriousness. Only after some time was he persuaded of the truth. The actual words he used on capitulation were typically generous of the man: 'I'll tell you what – I'll tell everyone who asks that you told me you caught them.' One can't ask fairer than that.

Nevertheless, experiences of this kind do give one a certain insight into human nature, and it's for· this reason that I've decided to publish these notes now. I'm going to set down *in advance* the details of my performance next year. I've just been planning it and it's quite clear from the way things are shaping up that that's what I've got to do; it's the only way I'm going to be able to cut out the inevitable carping and quibbling when my catches are subsequently reported by the press.

So here you are, with only a brief genuflection to the great William Caine, who once set down his own season in advance as well. The only detail I will omit will be the exact locations of the events described. We all know that gawping crowds and fine fishing do not mix.

The fact is that next year, between late April and the end of September, I intend to catch more trout in a single season than I have ever caught before. Let me come right into the open: I shall catch more trout than anyone else has caught before in a single season, anywhere, ever. Somewhere between 25,000 and 30,000 seems about right. I feel under no pressure to be more specific than that.

On the big lakes – Grafham, Chew, Rutland Water – where the bag limit is supposed to be eight fish and the average catch is less than one, I shall by a dispensation I plan to arrange catch at least eight fish at every visit, all of them over three pounds. Some visits I shall catch 28. On June 26th I am scheduled to get 103 trout and on August 5th, a further 122.

I am even prepared to tell you what conditions on the latter days will be like. Impossible. The temperature will be 83 Fahrenheit (or even Centigrade); the sun will beat like a brazier from overhead and no breath of air shall disturb the surface.

All of my fish on these days will be caught at 30 yards' distance, on 2lb breaking-strain points. They will have sipped in size 16 dry flies.

At the moment I intend that August 5th will be my best day, but some people – and they know who they are – shouldn't bank on it. I'll be taking a close interest in the catch returns and if I find them claiming improbable bags in an attempt to cap my own innocent openness, then I'll throw all restraint to the winds. In fact if that happens, I'll definitely go out on the last day of the season. I do not intend to reveal here what that day's catch will be. Suffice it to say that it will be adequate.

Insofar as fish sizes are concerned, I shall also do moderately well. Indeed, my season will encompass the lake records for both rainbow trout and brown.

Although rainbow trout have not been thought to exceed 20lbs in the wild in Britain, my new record fish will astonish everyone – though not, of course, myself – by tipping the scales at 62lbs exactly. It may lose a little before it can be weighed officially, but I shall not quarrel about an ounce or two.

River trout – and I give them fair warning now – are going to have a very hard time. My best trout from a river – a fish of 5lbs 7oz that is now fixing me with a beady eye from the wall above my desk – will not be evicted this year and how could anyone expect it to be? To suggest such a feat would strain credulity. But I will come close, very close; 5lbs 5oz, 5lbs 4oz and 5lbs 2oz (twice).

The best of these fish I shall take on my birthday. That's coincidence, I know, but we must accept these things when they happen. One thing no-one can do yet, thank God – microprocessor or no microprocessor – is to tell a trout when it can and cannot rise!

I will take this trout at the peak of the mayfly hatch, after everyone else has tried him and failed. It will be obvious to me that he's the only fish in the river not feeding on the carpet of mayflies all around, but has become fixated on a sparse – and uniquely late – hatch of February Duns. I shall tie on one of the February Duns only a fool would be without in late May and he'll have it first throw. As I said, 5lbs 5oz. Of course, I shall put him back.

Probably.

The most difficult fish of my season – perhaps the least easy is a more honest way to describe it – will be lying under an overhanging branch on the middle Kennet. He'll be tight into the bank where the current from a particular sidestream cuts viciously in, ready to drag a fly alarmingly across the surface the moment it is cast. But in truth there'll be no room to scratch your nose, let alone to backcast. The branches of the trees behind me will be reaching down my collar and there'll be a howling downstream gale. I'd guess it at Force 11, though it's notoriously difficult to be precise about these things.

Suddenly the fluke in the wind that I've been waiting for will coincide with a sudden, calming upthrust of water from a hitherto unseen weedbed. I shall have a split-second to act and I'll seize it coolly. I shall perform a rollcast using only the last two feet of my rod, the fly will weave its way uncannily through the branches and carry the leader behind it, tangle-free.

Walter Mitty – no bad performer himself with a rod – could not do it better, though I say so myself.

The fly will alight like a maiden's kiss, the trout will have it in a flash and his first plunging run will take him out of his lie and into open water where I can play him safely. Three pounds fourteen ounces, that one will go.

So much for the trout. But there's one other point about this next season that I'll mention because it troubles so many fly fishers: the coarse fish plague.

This year, I shall mistake no rising coarse fish for trout. Every trout I throw to will be a trout. Except one, and that will be a dace: 3lbs 10oz. The fact that this fish will more than double the ancient record will not excite me. I shall make no claim. To claim a record for a dace when one had initially thought the fish was a trout just wouldn't be on. We all have our lines to draw somewhere.

So there, then, just a few of the highlights of my season to come. They've not been easy to plan in such detail, but nothing's worth having that's not worth working for and anyway, I regard the effort as investment. It would certainly be possible to put up with all the carping, but one can't let one's credibility go.

Interpreting Riseforms

I have discussed elsewhere (see Trout Feeding Behaviour, page 70) how there is a relationship between a movement of the water and the manner of movement of the fish which makes it – and how there is a similar relationship between the movement of the trout and the creature it is trying to eat. It is these cause-and-effect links which provide the first clues when we are seeking to understand riseforms. Because different insects move differently and some insects (for example, dead ones) do not move at all, fish are obliged to move in sometimes quite distinctive ways, when they are feeding. These distinctive movements can be analysed to great advantage. FROM *The Times*, May 25, 1994.

While water is displaced in a host of ways when fish are rising, careful observation will show that a number of riseform types is repeatedly seen. Let us look at each of the most common in turn, to see what can be deduced.

One of the most common and fascinating of riseforms is a pinpoint ebbing of rings accompanied by an audible sipping or kissing noise. So tiny is this riseform that quite often the noise is heard first and it is only then that the tiny rings, the ebbing full-stop, is observed. Such a noise can only be caused by a fish sucking in air and the insect being eaten must therefore be in or on the surface film, because that is where the air is.

Because the rise is right at the surface and the disturbance is so small and specific, the fish must be moving slowly and with precision. A fish will only move with leisured precision on an insect it wants to eat, if instinct tells it the creature cannot get away. Flies at the surface that cannot get away are dead or dying – or else they are insects that have become trapped deep in the surface film by their struggles to break free.

The first artificial flies to think about when the sip rise is seen and heard and the naturals are about are olive spinners, because olive spinners characteristically collapse and die in the surface, after they have laid their eggs. The next artificials to consider are those suggesting other insects that can end up dead or trapped at the surface – among them midges, sedges and terrestrial flies. Whichever is opted for and whatever pattern is chosen, it should be fished in the surface film and not on it. The simplest way to achieve this is not to immerse the whole artificial in a bottle of flotant, but to apply one of the grease-type flotants to the back of the fly.

At the other extreme among riseforms, the angler sees a violent displacement of the surface, sometimes with water being thrown into the air and the body of the fish being glimpsed. Such a disturbance is clearly caused by a fish hitting the surface so hard that its momentum has carried it through.

A movement of this vigour is usually provoked by a large, live insect on the surface film or a large, mobile one in or immediately under it. Imitations of adult sedge flies, damsel flies and daddy-long-legs fished on the surface are the first patterns to try if the natural insects are about. Some adult sedges scutter over on the surface after hatching and again when laying their eggs; damsel flies hover temptingly close to the surface and sometimes land on it. Poor old daddy-long-legs is helpless on the water at any time. Sometimes, in a wind, daddy-long-legs flies will be bundled over and over like pieces of tumbleweed and fish chasing after them will cause eruptions.

Sedge pupae and damsel fly nymphs are the next general line of attack and they should be twitched briskly close to the surface, to suggest the movement of the natural creatures.

In a third riseform the back of the fish – but specifically not its mouth – will break the surface in a smooth, porpoising roll. Because the mouth is the business-end of the trout and does not break the surface, the fish is clearly taking something either hanging from the underside of the surface or just a fraction beneath it. On lakes, midge pupae waiting to break through the surface film to hatch are a common cause of this riseform; on rivers, midge pupae or smuts or spent olive spinners drifting immediately under the surface are often the cause. All artificials, including the olive spinner, should be fished within an inch of the surface to this riseform.

A fourth common riseform that is caused not by a fish at the surface but by one some way below it, is the 'boil' or 'bulging' rise. In this rise there is no sound and the fish is not seen. All that is seen is a sudden, domed welling-up or similar sharp distortion of the water that in a ripple can stun the surface and cause a calm patch to appear. Such a disturbance can only be caused by a fish turning briskly some way down. Fast-moving or awkwardly-moving insects will normally cause a feeding fish to move like this below the surface. So, often, will the excited feeding of shoals of fish that have come upon a heavy, upward migration of nymphs or pupae.

Artificials to try when this behaviour is seen are olive nymphs and sedge and midge pupae. If no result is forthcoming, damsel fly nymphs should be offered. These imitations should, of course, be fished below the surface which is where the natural insects are active and, on lakes, should be pulled a foot or two from time to time to suggest life. If these retrieves fail, faster or slower variations should be tried.

There is one other common riseform, less easily characterised than the other four, that I will call the 'ordinary' riseform. This riseform shows as substantial rings on a river, sometimes as a low-key surface swirl on a lake. Quite often a part of the fish shows, including the mouth. In this rise the fish is clearly taking something right off the surface and the prey is not large enough or moving fast enough to cause the fish to move at high speed. Rises like this are most often to olive duns, winged midges, small sedge flies and small terrestrial flies. A study of the surface and the air about may – as when assessing all other riseforms – suggest which one. The appropriate artificial dry fly, fished on and not in the surface, mostly without movement, sometimes with a sudden, attention-getting twitch, is the medicine.

And there we have it.

I would not want to imply from all of the above that the reading of riseforms is a clinical business, giving results that are measurable in microns. It is not. On the day, with water on the move and reflections and anxiety and frustration doing their stuff, one riseform can seem very much like another. Then our fallibility, or the marvellous cussedness of fish, will remind us which is boss.

But the general principles discussed here are sound and will be confirmed by any fly fisher with the willpower to stop fishing and watch from time to time. They will provide that most satisfying of starting points for the beginner and the old hand who so far has struggled: a sense of purpose in tying on one fly in preference to another, and in fishing it in one way instead of another.

The sudden revelation when it all comes together, can be as though a blinding light. On that Damascan road, there will be no turning back.

Trout in the Green-hazed Tunnel

Remember when? And that other day, close to the island where the bank sloped down? And what about those fish that night by the promontory, when the bats were out and one flew into the line?

The green-hazed tunnel, looking back, is lit with incident. There are all kinds of happenings down there: some so vivid and solid we could reach out and touch them, some oddly ethereal, like memory-ghosts. Every one of them, to have lasted so long, must have had something special about it: perhaps some coincidence of time and place, perhaps of novelty and atmosphere.

We all have such memories. Here are three of my own. I drew them together for a book of essays by different writers that had a unifying, geographical theme. FROM *West Country Fly Fishing* (1983).

It's not that I know the West Country well or even that I manage to get to it often. It's the quality of experience that I've had on those big wide lakes and soaked up in those intimate, pleated valleys that stirs me to write these notes.

What magic some of the names conjure up: Chew and Blagdon, Tamar and Exe, Taw and Torridge; and the little rivers – the Barle, the Lyd, the Carey; names that, over the years, have drawn me and others like me across those far-flung hills and along those winding, early-morning roads from London and

Hampshire and further afield, on the promise of a few days' (or even a single day's) sport. Somerset, Devon and Cornwall have given me some of the most vivid angling memories that I possess.

I remember an afternoon on Chew Valley Lake, many years ago. It was about three o'clock on a blazing August day and my companion and I sat listless in a boat, deep in a bay; suffocated, burdened by the heat that bore down.

We fished monotonously, mechanically; each without hope, each locked away in his drowsing cocoon, hermetically sealed. We'd caught nothing, we knew we were going to catch nothing but still, after the journey we'd had, we couldn't bring ourselves to call it a day.

And then, a hundred yards away, there was a splash: just the one but enough, as any angler will understand, to break into our numbed reverie, pull our eyes around and zoom them in like lenses, to focus on the spot where the ebbing rings oiled out.

A few moments later the surface rocked again and what seemed to be a thousand darts shot into the air. While they were still aloft a great trout slashed wildly at the surface and then, as our jaws fell open and our rods dropped lifeless to the gunwales, an entire shoal of trout hit the surface. In an instant we knew what we were about to witness, though neither of us had seen it before: a pack of marauding fish attacking a shoal of fry. The violence of it, seen in ever more detail as the turmoil drew nearer, left us awed and gaping; Mother Nature red in tooth and gill.

Every ten seconds or so the water exploded, as though Neptune's vast arm had thrown a cauldron of fry at the sun. Relentlessly the trout smashed in, now rending the water's surface, now bow-waving just beneath it; now concentrating the maelstrom of fry into a tighter group, for all the world like hunting dogs, before ramming themselves in again to cut out their prey; and now again, between attacks and roundings-up, lolloping head-first across the surface to pick up the maimed and the dead.

It went on for what seemed like an age. Before it was over the Roman circus had passed us by and was on its way out of sight. Around us, carnage lay everywhere. Trembling rings ebbed out from a thousand tiny fishes, gradually getting fainter with life itself.

Belly-up they lay, or spasmodically jerking along on their sides; some apparently regaining a lost consciousness, others instinctively, futilely, trying to swim, to put power into a tail that had become separated from the brain by a broken back.

It was like the aftermath of some great bomb, viewed distantly from space. So stunning was the spectacle, so awesome the result, that in all that time I don't think either of us threw a line.

The second incident also occurred in Somerset, also on a lake; though this time I was alone, down in a bay, fishing from the bank. It was in the early days, when I knew even less than I do now about what might possibly be the cause of what.

And it was night. The sun had gone down to my left through an opal sky, the world had stopped breathing and the fish had come up. All of them. Every fish in the lake. In my bay.

In a lifetime one sees a very few such rises. This was my first. I think I know now what I didn't know then: that those seemingly numberless head-and-tailing trout were besotted by an immense migration of ascending and hatching midge pupae.

Whatever the cause of the attention, the fish seemed oblivious to everything else as they stitched slow, undulating, meandering lines across the still surface in front of me and slurped and wallowed and rolled. Certainly they were oblivious to my fly as, in fading light, I cast in ever-greater desperation – first at this ring and then that, gradually becoming more and more frustrated, altering the direction of the throw from one riseform to another in mid-air, manufacturing a brand of aerialised spaghetti.

And then came the image that haunts me: the memory of a vast brown trout which adopted me and began to feed right down in front of me, beside my waders. I can't honestly say whether I saw it first or felt it – but so close did it happen that it could have been either: a movement in the water, close enough to touch. I looked down in time to see the great broad spade of a tail disappear from sight not a foot away. And then I saw it followed immediately by the head and shoulders as the trout began another porpoising roll, and then another and another, moving in a circle around me not three feet away.

All across the bay other fish were rising, too. As I fished on, ever more frenziedly, it turned into a nightmare; like some awakening after death to a world of trout and then, after a brief moment's joy, having the elation crushed out by a wave of awareness that one was in some fly fisher's hell, doomed to be tormented and teased by feeding fish, close enough to be lifted from the water but destined never to succumb.

I pointed my rod to the sky and dribbled whatever confection I had on the point onto the water beside me, skating it around the head of my own fish, the trout that I could see but which was utterly oblivious to me. But to no avail. He simply went on rising beside me in a world that began with this fly and ended with the next, the gentle ripples he made lapping against my leg, rolling between my waders. He wasn't disdainful, he wasn't contemptuous, he wasn't anything. I was neither relevance nor irrelevance: my fly, my frustration, my aching, my very self simply did not exist.

And then, after I suppose three or four minutes, he departed: he simply followed his tilting nose off into the nearby night, feeding uninterrupted all the while.

And was gone.

It was an experience that crushed me utterly and which haunts me still.

I have another memory of the West Country. It is of the little River Lyd during the great drought of 1976. That was the year when, in most parts of Britain, no rain fell at all between April and October; and in July that small stream, never anything of tidal proportions, wrinkled its way down the parched brown valley like a withered vein.

I was there to fish for sea trout. Miraculously, some had wriggled their way up where the water creaked its way through the stones in the shallows; and now, during the day, they lay in the few pools which remained, sheltering beneath the trees and the high overhanging banks.

Sea trout fishing, as any sane man knows, is an evening and night-time pursuit and so, with the temperature in the eighties,

I set off at three in the afternoon to try for one with the nymph.

A little way downstream from the bridge I found her. I'd crawled Indian-style through the high vegetation and worked my way cautiously through the branches of an overhanging tree, to look down from the cliff bank. And there she was, lying in front of a rock at the downstream edge of a long, deep pool where the bed sloped sharply up.

A few feet away the small, street-wise trout of the West Country, the urchins rather than the lords of the stream, drifted alertly from side to side, now darting forward to intercept something ahead, now waste-not-want-not sliding swiftly up and to one side to take the occasional surface fly.

But the sea trout did nothing. She simply lay there like a great grey shade; a submarine ghost against the pebbles of the bottom, motionless.

My word but she was big!

I watched her for a long time – perhaps half an hour, perhaps more; I've spent far longer than that watching undisturbed fish just being fish. I came to know her intimately, as one always does; noticing, as one always does, that she wasn't really motionless at all. I noticed the slow twinkling fan of a tail that held her on station upstream of the rock and how, imperceptibly, like a tethered kite, she responded to the tiny ribbons of turbulence which anxiously pushed past her, eager to reach the sea before the stream finally dried up.

But eventually the hunter in me overcame the naturalist. I had to try to catch her. Cautiously I edged back along the bough I'd been lying on, crawled back from the bank to collect my rod and moved downstream.

I had to go down a long way before I could negotiate the steep bank and get down into the water – maybe 40 yards, maybe more. Then, slowly, I began to pick my way back. I was immensely careful, lifting my feet out of the water like a heron, vertically enough to leave a hole in the water where my legs had been, doing everything I could to avoid that fatal push of water upstream and its rolling and chinking semaphore sneak. Whenever my feet went down it was to grope and read the bottom, seeking stones that wouldn't move under my weight, crevices that wouldn't open up as the rocks moved aside, sending their muted thunder upstream to my quarry ahead. No man, I remember thinking, could have been more unobtrusive. Sombre clothing, matt-varnished rod, careful, gentle tread; I only just knew I was there myself.

Perhaps ten minutes those 25 yards took me, before I could see the rock and then the fish ahead of it.

Slowly I inched a yard or two more, brought the rod gingerly around from behind me and, looking at the fish all the while, groped up the cane with my left hand to unhitch the tiny, weighted fly.

One more yard, one more yard and it would be an easy throw. I dropped the nymph into the water to let the stream carry it behind me in preparation for the cast.

Now! Keeping the rod low I flicked it forward – and then an extraordinary thing happened. The fish, before that first forward movement of the line could straighten, began to dissolve before my eyes. One moment it was there, all distant composure; the next – the very instant I moved with evil but cautious intent – it began to disappear. Not with clouds of silt and rocking eddies, not with heaves at the surface and bow-waves behind. It simply dispersed, compactly; like someone walking off into a fog until you can't see him, can't see him, can't see him . . . any more.

And again, that's all. An event of consuming inconsequence. Simply a memory of a fish disappearing in a remarkable way when it shouldn't have been alarmed at all, shouldn't have known I was there at all. No dramatics, no heroics, no memorable struggle with my Moby Dick.

I've had those too, of course; at other times, on other days. But the memories of the West Country that I cherish most are made of subtler stuff: of images and atmospheres, incident and charm; and fishes and water and light.

Of the ether, as well as of the ethos, of the fly.

How to Tell Good Flies from Bad

Most anglers do not tie their own flies and so have to buy mass-produced, ready-made dressings from the shops. The market for such dressings is vast. The boxes in the tackle shops are so crammed, pulse and radiate so brightly that they should, one might think, be kept under dark glass. Many shop-bought flies have been tied at breakneck speed using cheap materials because the price at which they must be delivered to the dealer, for selling on, is critical.

The trade, quite naturally, offloads the lot. The best are selected by those who know what they are looking for, even if they do not tie their own. The rest go to the unwary and undiscriminating – which means beginners, who need all the help they can get, and those older hands who, for this reason or that, have taken no great interest in what makes a fly effective. Knowing the difference between a good fly and a dud fly can make the difference between a rise and no rise, a bag and nothing. Here are some points to look for.
FROM *The Times*, May 17, 1995.

It is rubbing-hands-together-and-chortling-like-Fagin time. It is 'how about this and isn't that a beauty and if you haven't got a dozen of these it isn't worth going' time. Spring is the time when tackle dealers see the fly fisher coming and offload enough coloured confections to stock a rainforest with parakeets.

I never did meet a fly fisher who was not a sucker for a new

189

fly, any more than I ever met a coarse fisher who was not a sucker for a new float. Show me a tackle bag and I will show you excess baggage. Do not look into anything of mine.

For the old hand who buys almost as a tribute to the tackle dealer's pitch, all of this is fair enough. He knows that flies for collecting and flies for fishing with are not the same thing.

For the newcomer and the untutored it can be a different matter. They are meat to the trade and it roasts them. For the gullible, fly choice equals fly bewilderment, fly bewilderment equals sales opportunity, sales opportunity equals sales pitch, sales pitch equals purchase. Naturally, purchase does not equal fish.

So where does the trout man begin? How does he avoid the useless and buy the effective? What are the characteristics of a killing fly?

I know of no rules of thumb for lures and the small flasher patterns characterised by many traditional loch flies: trout will take all kinds of things below the surface and much is influenced by the way such flies are moved. The only rules that apply to nymphs is that they should look like the kind of small, rather drab naturals which trout eat and that they should be moved, generally (though there are exceptions) in a food-like way, which is to say, slowly. There are, though, a few rules of thumb which apply to dry flies. To apply these rules it is necessary to understand something of the principles of dry fly design. They are based on an understanding of what trout see when they look up at a fly.

The best fly designers have always known that the finest creations they can produce look pathetic compared to natural insects because the differences scream out. They have also long understood that feeding trout are not comparing artificial with natural and looking for differences.

All experience suggests that a trout is programmed to respond to similarities. If it sees a lot of natural flies on the water, it recognises the familiar signals they send out. It has lived all its life by responding to such signals and when it sees them it reacts by recognising food.

The art of the fly dresser is based on this reaction and is not unlike the art of the cartoonist. When a cartoonist shows us

certain features – often wildly exaggerated features – of a politi-
cian, we respond with 'Mr Big!' even though the pen-strokes on
the paper look nothing like Mr Big in reality.

In designing an effective dry fly, the fly dresser is suggesting
and exaggerating the signals that a natural fly standing on the
surface transmits below the surface. Let us consider them.

The natural fly is on the surface, it has a particular colour, is
of a given size and it creates tiny impressions in the surface where
its feet, its body and sometimes its wings touch the film. When a
hungry trout sees such impressions it is likely to rise because of
these signals alone: every surface insect it has ever taken has
displayed them in a broadly similar way. From time to time a
particularly wary fish – say one that has been pricked before –
might look at a fly longer and more carefully; but in the main the
principal signals seem to be enough.

It is on the basis of these few features alone that the most
successful dry flies – for rivers especially – are designed. They are
flies which match the sizes of natural insects – and that mostly
means flies on hook sizes 18, 16, 14 and 12. They are flies which
have broadly the right colour. They are flies that in the main are
dressed as sparsely as is consistent with the need to float because,
in the main, natural flies are slender and dainty and lacking in fuzz.

On lakes the wise fly dresser will take an additional factor into
account. While on rivers the current brings the fly to the fish, in
lakes the trout must go in search of the fly – and so visibility must
be considered. As I remark elsewhere, while it does not follow
that because a fish sees a fly it will take it, it certainly is true that
no fish will take a fly it has not seen.

Two other small but important points should be noted.
Unless the fish are small and are to be pursued with light tackle,
fine-wire hooks should be avoided. Fine-wire hooks are pushed
no end by the trade for dry flies and most commercially-tied dries
are dressed on them. But fine-wire hooks are prone to open,
especially on the strike and in weedy water where sizeable fish
swim. Too often they lead to losses.

The second point is that the hackle for a good dry fly should
extend only a fraction beyond the gape of the hook. Most shop-

bought artificials are tied with hackles like flue-brushes. They project two, three and even four times the width of the gape. Such enormous hackles do not only make hooking more difficult, they much diminish the chances of a rise in the first place: being so large, they do not send out signals consistent with the signals transmitted by the small natural insects they are supposed to represent.

Short-fibred hackles are much more expensive than long because there are relatively few of them on the average cape; and flies tied with them are therefore more expensive, too. They are an investment worth making.

Common Bonds

I find it impossible to walk across a bridge without looking over, or to see someone fishing without stopping to watch. My friends are all the same. So, I suspect, are most anglers. We are lookers-in and lookers-on by nature, if we cannot be fishing ourselves. The same bonds bind, the same elements bewitch, whatever kind of fishing we do. FROM *The Times*, August 22, 1992.

It is no coincidence that angling is so popular. Indeed, it has so many attractions, can appeal on so many levels at so many ages to so many temperaments, that it could hardly be otherwise.

One of the sport's special qualities is that it can seal off and seal in; it can absorb and transport utterly, regardless of place and time and circumstance. I have just seen the spell cast three times on the same day.

In the morning I fished one of the loveliest stretches of trout stream in England. For 100 years and more it has been crafted for fly fishing. The water has been controlled and channelled, the banks have been sculpted and manicured. Indolent trout lie out everywhere in full and provocative view.

They are expensive fish. My host pays thousands of pounds a year for his rod there, say hundreds a week and even hundreds a day. Umpteen pounds an hour. Umpteen pounds a fish. Yet to the amusement of my friend and the astonishment of the keeper, I spent much of the time ignoring the trout and concentrating on coarse fish. Say umpteen for an old-fashioned penny.

We had started with the trout but by lunchtime I had caught enough. There was no challenge. The water was so heavily stocked I imagined the fish dare not jump out for fear of not getting back in.

After lunch, leaving my friend asleep under a tree and the keeper still in his cottage, I walked far down the bank and came on uncharted land. From the moment I reached the huge back-water, I was mentally lost. The banks there had been left to grow wild, to act as a screen against a right of way. The river there had been left to grow wild, also.

The water, when I managed to make my way to it, was deep and clear. High fronds of weed, lush and green, orchestrated a faint current. In a break in the weed, suspended mid-water, there was a shoal of fish. One fish turned and winked soft silver light. Its fins were an orange-red. It was a pristine fish, a roach; and on that instant I was 10 years old again, playing in the wood and beside the stream, wide-eyed and spellbound.

For a long time I forgot my rod, for far longer still I forgot the trout. The more I looked, the more I melted into the time lagoon at my feet.

A gang of large perch, broad-shouldered and flashy, shrugged and muscled their way down the pool like wide boys out on the razzle. A herd of bream appeared nose-down from some lily-pads and grazed and cropped the bottom, rummaged in the silt, stirred up cumulus clouds of brown. A chub, a monstrous fish, bronze and barrel-fat, slid purposefully by.

And time passed. The sun burned, the trout dimpled and the landscaped park lay splendid before me, all unremarked. It was the roach that absorbed. Of course, I had to give them a try.

There was no room to cast. The bushes behind beckoned my rod, the reeds in front would magnetise any stray hook. I had to dibble. I parted the reeds as carefully as I could and insinuated the rod-tip through them. Fins quickened; a couple of fish turned full-circle in little more than their body-lengths and then settled again. I lowered the rod and let the weighted nymph on the end of the leader, sink down.

Nine trout out of 10 would have had that fly on its first twinkling fall; one trout in any group would have lunged forward and grabbed it lest a neighbour got there first.

194

But not the roach, not then and not for a long time. Time after time the wild and wily, umpteen-to-a-penny fish parted to let the nymph through, then closed their ranks. They proved as much a test of my mettle that day as dace and chub had done when I was a boy. I tried ever-smaller nymphs and ever-finer leaders. I varied the weights and varied the colours and eventually persuaded one of the smaller fish to take.

It was only when I lifted the rod and felt the weight and let out a joyous whoop that I realised I was not alone. My friend and the keeper, unnoticed beneath a nearby alder, broke into mock applause. They had been there, they said, for at least 15 minutes and I had been missing for nearly an hour.

That evening, my drive home took me through a town with a canal through its centre. I caught a glimpse of someone fishing, glanced at my watch and pulled over and stopped.

A youth of 19 or 20 was sitting by the side of the canal, float-fishing. There was a footpath immediately behind him and a municipal park behind that. Small boys ran and wrestled, old men stretched uncertain legs, women bustled, couples canoodled. And oblivious to it all the young man sat on his tackle-box casting out, reeling in, occasionally slipping a tiny silver bleak into a keep-net that would have held a shark.

All the world seemed intent on distracting him. It came in ones and twos and family groups, sometimes with inquisitive dogs. There were the mildly curious, the amused and bemused, the titterers, the stoppers and talkers. One man turned angling first into a spectator sport, then into a joint experience. He settled cross-legged beside the concentrating youth, neither speaking nor being spoken to, sharing the young angler's float. He was still there when I left. So was the young angler, undistracted by any of it, fishing on as though utterly alone.

The walk back to my car took me to the bridge over which most of the evening traffic roared. Juggernauts ground and groaned, cars idled and inched, radio music fused to cacophony through a hundred wound-down windows; fumes shimmered in the hot, still air. The bridge itself was sprayed with graffiti – Jim and Tracy, Mods are Back, Maggie Out and the rest: old stuff.

There was a tiny patch of grass on the far side of the bridge, before the path curled away into what looked like an industrial estate. It was just big enough for the man sitting in the collapsible chair.

He had a fishing rod beside him, a box full of spools and tins, a loaf of bread close to hand, clearly his bait. He had no float. His line ran straight down into the water and his gaze was fixed intently on his rod-end waiting for it to tremble and signal a bite. He did not notice me.

Even in that soulless place beneath that dome of noise, the man in the collapsible chair was quite as complete, every bit as sealed off as the lad in the park who had been sharing the float, every bit as sealed in as I had been with my roach.

If the three of us had fished together we would have understood one another completely. The same bonds bound us, the same elements bewitched. No wonder we are so thick on the ground.

Casting off the Edge of the World

It must have been as a boy that the name first stuck. I do not know what the map was, if it was a map; or who the author was, if it was a book, but it seems as though the name has always been there, lodged in my imagination like a flaming arrow. Tierra del Fuego! Land of Fire! What images the name conjures up. Volcanoes, maybe, and red, spilling lava; or natives on a headland, silhouetted against flames. In my mind, in many minds, ·the name is synonymous with the remotest place the imagination can grasp. Tierra del Fuego, the very end of the world.

Nothing much can change in that extraordinary place, nothing much about it can alter. Jets, though, are bringing it nearer. Now flights carrying anglers arrive there most weeks in the Southern autumn before the hounds of Cape Horn slip their leash. The planes come down from Buenos Aires, partly over coast, partly over hazed deserts. They touch down at Rio Grande airport at the mouth of the Rio Grande river, the most famous sea trout river in the world.

I once fished the Rio Grande for a week. It was a week that came flooding back to me, in tiny detail, long afterwards, thanks to a mishap in the post. FROM *The Times*, January 1, 1996.

M y young grandson was thrilled with his new car transporter. He was playing with it when he asked if Father Christmas had come to my house, too. As it happens, Father Christmas did come. He popped a small package through my letter box. It contained what a film processing laboratory had long since claimed it had never received: a set of transparencies shot in Tierra del Fuego.

The pictures cleared away the haze of distance and time. One brought back every detail of one of the most memorable hour's fishing that I have ever had. Another provided proof-positive of a sea trout beyond imagining.

It is a long time since I fished the Rio Grande. The river lies like a crack across the coccyx of South America's spine. It flows through desolately beautiful, limitlessly horizoned plains, more or less due east from the Andes. It empties into the South Atlantic, more or less midway between the Magellan Straits and Cape Horn.

I fished from Kau-Tapen lodge, 20 miles inland on a rolling dirt road. There were six of us there: three Argentinians, two Americans and me. We fished singly or in pairs, always with a professional guide armed with spare flies and a vast landing net that had a powerful spring balance built into the handle.

The fishing, in spite of the renowned size of the Rio Grande's sea trout, was all with single-handed trout rods. I used a seven-weight, nine-foot carbon rod equipped with a butt extension to take some strain off my wrist, a large-capacity disc-braked reel and, most of the time, a weight-forward, fast-sinking line.

The line had as much to do with the wind as the water. The Rio Grande is easily wadable on most reaches and most of the water is briskly-paced, perfect for the fly. In calm weather, a floating line would have been a delight to use; but, when I was there, the wind blew almost without relent. It became a living, bullying thing. It whistled about my rod as though through a ship's rigging, it flapped my waterproofs about my head like loose sails. The wind whipped tears from my eyes, impressed itself on my cheeks, moved the very ears on my head when it gusted from behind.

When the wind was up, the narrow, heavy sinking line was needed as much to help me cast as to sink close to the bottom.

It was, though, part of the experience: the challenge was to work with the wind and not to struggle against it.

When the wind dropped, which it did from time to time, we shared the high, wide skies with spiralling condors and noise-some flights of Magellan geese. We shared the honey-coloured plains with honey-coloured guanacos, llama-like animals that studied us hair-triggered, edgily curious. We shared the water with the muskrats and the beavers and the fish.

My fear had been that I would arrive too soon; that coming in early January in a season that runs from January to the end of March would see me miss the main runs. Yet the river was already full of fish, now rolling and sploshing, now winking silver, now sullenly lying doggo in the long, wide pools.

There are rivers quite like the River Grande in Alaska: wide sweeps of rivers that are filled with salmon from bed to surface and bank to bank when the height of the season comes; but, in Alaska at these times, the fishing is easy. It can be a fish each cast and it is not so much the energy that needs to be paced, but the day.

Here, although there were fish in great numbers, they were more dispersed and had to be worked for. We each caught our share, but they were mostly hard-won.

And what fish! In most rivers in Great Britain that contain sea trout the fish average around one pound, approaching maybe two. A three-pounder is a nice one, friends hear of four-pounders, five-pounders are noted on Christmas cards to old angling enemies.

In six full days and one evening on the Rio Grande, I caught 23 sea trout – by no means an exceptional score. The smallest weighed 5lbs. The average was just a fraction under 10lbs. The largest was – well, very large.

The fish came at first in ones and twos, the daily score gradu-ally creeping up as the week progressed, which is the proper way for any fishing week to unfold.

There were many memorable fish. There was the great fish that leapt clean onto the distant bank to take its bearings when it was hooked, and that then leapt immediately back into the water ready for the fight. There was the fish that leapt above my head while I was wading chest-deep and that trailed rubies behind it through the red, setting sun.

Above all there were the fish in the photographs: the one recalling a moment in the best day I had, the other freezing forever that sea trout of my lifetime.

The best day began on a long pool with a high bank opposite. It was, my guide said, usually fished from the near bank at the upstream end. I said that for all the awkwardness of the high bank for casting, I favoured the side opposite, at the pool's lower end. To some head-shaking and what I like to think was mere tut-tutting in Spanish, I waded over. With the first cast, I hit a fish that shattered the surface at once and came off. Second cast, I had a solid pull but failed to connect. Third cast, I had a take so violent that it pulled my heart into my mouth.

I stumbled and splashed downstream behind an unseen force, tripped over a branch that lay white and bleached as an old bone and eventually landed the trout. We slipped out the barbless hook, my American companion took the photograph of the sea trout, my guide and me that I am looking at now – and then we returned the prize to the water, as we did with every catch that week. It had weighed 13lbs.

I made my way back to the same casting spot. Another cast, another thumping take, another rod-creaking, breathless fight. A ten-pounder. Next cast, a missed fish. The cast after that, a fish that took with such immense, sudden power that I found myself looking at a shattered line streaming head-high, downwind.

A new leader, a new fly, a new cast and a new fish, a cart-wheeling seven-pounder that was 30 yards downstream before I could gather up the loose line and follow. All of this, all of it, in less than an hour and still another 13-pounder and another five-pounder to come.

The great fish came on my last day. It came from the neck of a deep, fast pool: a broad-shouldered, barrel-chested monster of a fish that was impossibly thick right down to the tail. It took forever to land, time after time turning away from the net and bow-waving across the shallows towards the middle; but eventually he tired. I laid the fish gently on the grass, put my rod beside it to give some measure of scale, and took out my camera. Click. Seventeen pounds precisely.

That fish was as exhausted as I was. I can see myself now nursing it back to strength, holding it upright facing the current. I begin to feel it flex and shrug, see its pectoral fins gradually extend and splay; watch as it gulps oxygen steady and slow; and then the great tail sweeps aside my holding hands and the fish is gone, heading for its destiny in the foothills of the Andes.

So yes, I told my grandson, Father Christmas did come to my house this year. He came in a blue uniform, in broad daylight, on a bicycle; and he brought me a transporter, too.

A Corker

I have never disturbed the slumbers of the Record Fish Committee. Though I have in my time fished very hard and intensely, I have always been more interested in the problems of how and why than of what: in challenge and difficulty than in pure size.

These days I am generally less intense. I still think about my fishing a lot and if the fish are moving – especially if they are moving on top – I will fish as concentratedly as anyone. But I do not attack the water or sublimate all else to my fishing any more.

Even so, from time to time, I find myself attached to a corker. Most people who spend enough time at the water, do. The biggest fish I ever caught, relatively speaking, was a grayling. FROM *The Sunday Times*, November 25, 1984.

'To catch a big fish, first find a big fish' has always been sound advice. I recently found one. A week later I caught it and achieved one of the more modest goals I set myself in youth: to get a weighed, measured, witnessed, no hanky-panky grayling topping two pounds.

As it turned out the fish did not simply top two pounds and then go some: it went beyond the size where sensible men stop dreaming lest they awake ranting in the night. It went – let me delay no longer – to within an ace of 3lbs.

I do not know when my interest in grayling began but it goes far back. Maybe it had something to do with the way I caught my first, one Christmas morning from the River Tees at High Conniscliffe, when we had to push a raft of ice out of the little bay before we could start and the line kept freezing in the rod rings. Maybe it has been the beauty of the fish – slender, bright silver, lightly spotted and with that wonderful, lilac-tinged dorsal high on its back, big as spinnaker.

Maybe it is the curious nature of the fish. The grayling is such an odd cove. He has an adipose fin so he is one of the game fishes yet he is scaled like a coarse fish and breeds as though one. He is a kind of aristocrat conceived the wrong side of the blanket. He fights like neither fish nor fowl. Actually he fights like a cucumber in the current, an image I use not to detract from *Thymallus thymallus* but to describe how he feels when he is twisting on my line. He is as difficult as an eel to hold. When you try to unhook him he bends this way and that like a piece of sprung metal. He has that extraordinary, pear-shaped eye. He has that oddly underslung mouth.

Indeed, the grayling is so interesting and arouses such curiosity that it has a society devoted entirely to itself. The membership of the Grayling Society now runs to several hundreds. The society studies the grayling's natural history, amasses historical and current data on its sizes and distribution and works to rehabilitate it among the ranks of more respectable fish which have no doubts about their ancestries.

It is the question of size that puts the apparent modesty of a 2lb ambition in perspective. Countrywide, the grayling averages maybe 10 inches long and weighs 4oz. A one-pound fish is a nice one, a one-and-a-half pounder is a good one and a fish of a pound-and-threequarters is splendid. The thought of a two-pound grayling has some men – well, members of the Grayling Society, anyway – tossing restless abed.

Of course, it is not uncommon to find men who say they've caught a two-pounder. But such fish have rarely been weighed. They have even more rarely been weighed and witnessed. Scales and witnesses are the grim reapers of angling enthusiasm and essential adornments of a sport which, it is well known, is replete with folk who can catch specimens three at a time without ever leaving their bar-stools – yet who find it curiously more difficult on the riverbank when watched.

My own moment of weighed, witnessed, no hanky-panky glory came ·on September 23rd with not a bar-stool in sight. Indeed, it came at 12.45pm on September 23rd at a point just out from a bunch of bankside nettles growing out over a certain pool above a certain bend on a certain reach of a certain river somewhere (as they say) in southern England.

I had first found the fish the previous Sunday while stalking trout: vast submarine shades of grey and sepia which, if they are looked for hard enough can sometimes be seen drifting in-substantially in the deep, curling water there, close to the bank. He was exactly where I'd have expected a feeding trout to be: high in the water, drifting compactly from side to side and picking up nymphs and shrimps which the current had swept from the weedbeds above.

When I first saw an outline confused by turbulence, I thought of trout, not grayling. Then I moved a fraction too quickly on the skyline, the fish caught sight of me and turned quickly to the depths. There was a flash of silver, a wink of lilac from a dorsal fin that looked as big as a man's hand and a split-second, curiously slow-motion glimpse of a vanishing, deeply-forked tail.

Suddenly and unexpectedly I had 'first found my fish'. Everyone needs a little luck.

I knew he would not reappear that day and I also knew that I could not risk frightening him another time by approaching him again from the high bank. I was confident he would stay in the same place but any cast for him would have to be made blind, from the shallower water some way below. And if I was going to have to cast blind at some point in the future, I would have to mark his favoured position precisely, now.

It was not difficult. First I measured his position up the pool: a little over a rod's-length directly out from the bunch of nettles, just this side of a crinkle in the current.

Next, because the crinkle might have disappeared before I could return, I slipped into the water downstream, waded cautiously up and across the marled bottom to the best casting position I could find and then looked upstream, directly over the crinkle, to the bankside. Got it. The fish had been lying where a mental line drawn upstream to a clump of brambles trailing in the water, was intersected by a mental line drawn out from the nettles.

Next, tactics. A grayling of that size would not rise to the surface to take so I would have to use a pattern capable of sinking through the heavy current, to reach him. What weight of fly, when cast a given distance upstream of the fish, would have sunk to the depth of the fish in the water by the time the current had swept it back? And at exactly what point in the current upstream of the fish would the fly have to be dropped if the fly were to come back to the grayling not only correct for depth but correct for line, as well?

Exactly a week later I slipped into the water, made my way slowly to the casting position I had chosen, concentrated on a point in the current about 30ft upstream of the intersection of my two mental lines, and cast.

An artificial shrimp weighted with six turns of thin lead wire straightened an exceptionally long, fine leader and went in. I had chosen a long, fine leader to minimise resistance to the sinking fly and had greased the butt some distance from the hook to help me spot the offer.

Nothing happened. The fly came back close to where I had wanted it, but the leader showed no sign of movement. I cast again, this time a foot further to the right. Again the leader straightened, the fly came back to where the grayling might be – but again, nothing. Nor anything on the next cast.

On the fourth cast the leader flinched and then drew suddenly downwards as though the fly had snagged weed. I brought the rod up, made contact and for a joyous moment glimpsed lilac and silver.

Angling literature is full of torrid, palpitating accounts of battles with great fishes – the rod is always creaking, the reel is always screaming, there are the inevitable last-minute dashes for freedom – all of them described moment by moment. But as so often in my experience, it wasn't like that. One powerful run upstream into the depths of the pool, a searing rush downstream into the shallows below me; a nervous half-stumbling chase after him with the rod high to keep the line off the water and the water surging perilously off the prow of my waders and I had gained control.

A minute or two later, when he tried to rush downstream again with the heavy current on his spinnaker, I dropped my rod sharply left, his head turned and his own momentum beached him, carrying him in a fast, wide, sweeping curve onto the slope of a small gravel island. Before I could reach him the barbless size 10 had fallen out.

Back at the fishing hut he measured just seventeen and a half inches from the point of his nose to the cleft of his tail. But he was an incredible 2lbs 13oz on the scales. He was not only the biggest grayling anyone there had seen, he was also the fattest, with shoulders on him that would have done credit to a carp.

Later that week, when the scales were checked, virtue produced a proper reward. The scales were shown to weigh one ounce light and the fish was logged at 2lbs 14oz.

I sent scales from the fish to the Freshwater Fisheries Laboratory at Pitlochry, for interest. Expert reading showed the fish had been six years old. Given his length when caught he would at the end of his first winter have been about seven-and-a-half inches long; by the end of his second winter he would have grown to about fourteen-and-a-half inches long. Then, as is typical of grayling, his lateral growth had slowed dramatically – but he had gone on building up weight, especially on his shoulders.

The Grayling Society had authenticated records of only 23 fish of similar size and bigger being taken in the previous 50 years. Of these, only half a dozen had been taken on the fly.

It is just possible I will see a bigger grayling. From time to time very big fish do turn up – sometimes caught, sometimes found when rivers are electro-fished and netted. But I will not catch a bigger grayling, for sure. So he is going into a glass case. He will have his weight and measurements and date of capture on the front and for good measure an enlarged photograph of his revealing scale pinned to the back.

He will quite demonstrably be a weighed, measured and witnessed 2lb grayling. He will very nearly be a 3lb grayling – and no hanky-panky.

The Importance of Public Opinion

The angling press devotes much space to the issue of 'the antis' – to the problem of dealing with the threat posed by those who want to see our sport banned.

In my view, to focus on the antis is to misjudge the target. The antis are only relevant in the extent to which they can influence public opinion. It is towards the maintenance of public support that our efforts should be aimed. While we have the public at large behind us, we are safe. When their support starts to crumble on any scale – and it can be undermined as much by what we do ourselves as by what our opponents do – we are looking into the void.

There is a particular danger in the way the game-fishing press often addresses aspects of the issue. It frequently talks as though salmon, trout and sea trout exist in a vacuum. The catch-and-release debate, I think, illustrates this well.

Many have argued that the way to retain moral justification for what we do is to kill and eat our catch. Not to do so, they say, is to play into our opponents' hands. We are treating sentient creatures as playthings.

Whatever view one takes on matters like this – and there is little point in discussing the morality of angling because we either fish or we do not – the reality is that our greatest strength lies in our numbers. Sea anglers, who greatly outnumber game anglers, eat most of what they catch for the very good reason that it is good on the plate. Coarse anglers, who are counted in millions and who outnumber sea and game anglers combined, do not eat their catch for the very good reason that it is, in the main, inedible.

To argue, therefore, that anglers should fish for the pot or not at all – this is certainly not something the sea anglers have suggested – is effectively to subscribe to the ending of coarse fishing. It is a notion which, if widely held, would set angler against angler and cut game angling, which is divided even within its own ranks, adrift from its source of greatest strength: it would maroon us on an island of dubious self-justification where we could be attacked with much greater ease.

There are many other issues in the 'antis' debate. Some of them are more brutal and come much closer to home. Even though the issues referred to here are in a constant state of flux and move on and off the agenda from year to year, the attitudes underlying them seem always to be with us. FROM *The Field*, April, 1993.

I have in front of me a copy of a typed, A4 publication called *Pisces*. It is the newsletter of the Campaign for the Abolition of Angling. Under the heading 'Good Riddance' there appears the following: 'A well-known angler and ex-policeman was killed by a former colleague when a gun fractured at a duck shoot. Parts of him were not recovered, which should have pleased the fish and given them a free meal'.

When anglers debate the threat posed by the anti-angling faction, it is people capable of this kind of sentiment that they are often – though not always – discussing. Left on their own, I do not believe such folk would pose any significant danger to our sport. Indeed, the contrary: their sheer extremism alienates so much that they set back both their own cause and that of others who take a more moderate view.

Alas, we do not leave them alone to struggle on, unaided. Being anglers, we naturally give them help.

I have made a list of just some of the ways in which we are currently helping those who want to see our sport banned. Most of the items on it are initiatives taken by fishery owners who find themselves in an over-subscribed market and who need to do something – anything – to carve themselves a niche.

There are no items in this list that will be news to the Campaign for the Abolition of Angling. Indeed, the point in reproducing it is to list issues that are long-established; that have received extensive, uncritical exposure in some of the angling press (and sometimes much mindless hype); and moreover that have the support of sufficient fishermen to make them viable options.

For many years we have allowed the cynical manipulation of the trout records for commercial gain: a minority of fishery owners has hand-reared fish already over the long-recognised record weights and introduced them into small ponds where they cannot fail to be caught. It is a practice that has cheapened the sport's image outside and caused much anguished debate inside. To meet the new realities, new record lists have had to be created for each game species – one for 'natural fish' that have made most or all of their growth in the wild and one for stew-bred porkers. Over time, as more loopholes are seen and exploited, more lists are likely to prove necessary. It is not the fact that big fish are stocked that is the problem; big fish are no different in kind to medium fish and small fish. It is the engineering of records, the weaving in and out of the rules, that seems so pathetic and is so damaging.

Coarse fishing is not immune to cynical practices. Some coarse fishery owners overstock their lakes to such an extent that competition for food is created among the fish. The aim is to reduce the natural caution of fish when faced with a bait, thereby making the fishing easier. Easier fishing attracts more customers and the cash tills ring. Indeed, some overstock to such an extent that the fish can scarcely survive without anglers' groundbait. Perversity has been heaped upon perversity by owners who have used this situation as an argument for abolishing the close season, which takes anglers – and hence their groundbait and money – away.

Some coarse fishery owners have found another variation: they have effectively abolished the close season because they stocked token trout as the close season for coarse fish neared and then announced 'any method' trout fishing – a practice which has had as its sole aim the ability to allow angling to continue for spawning coarse fish which otherwise, by law, would have been protected.

Elsewhere, carp are reared to great size and then stocked in small lakes to be caught again and again on rods marketed under names like 'Top Gun' and 'Armalite'. When a fish has been caught enough times for the novelty to have worn off among the local chest-beaters on one lake, it is sometimes netted out and sold on to another fishery to be caught a few times more; and then sold on again and then again, the specific, relentless focus of scalp-hunters wherever it goes.

There are pike anglers and others who still persist in using live-baits. Many fly-fishing competitions have been based on a kill-all policy, a practice which has led to scores of stiff, dried carcasses being paraded along the banks, with competitors happily posing among them for the press. Live fish in coarse angling competitions are sometimes treated abominably, as anyone who goes to one can see.

There are many other such examples.

Now here is the nub. If there are two seeds deeply sown in our national psyche they are a sense of fair play and a love of animals. Scratch any one of us and you will find them there. So while I do not believe those in the anti-faction would be any danger on their own, the activities of a minority of fishery owners and anglers are providing motivation, food, drink and propaganda for them in the only battle that matters: the battle for public opinion.

Currently, public opinion is on our side. It is one of our great strengths that the non-angling community sees angling, in the main, as a guileless and mildly idiosyncratic pursuit. Selectively presented as the generality, however – and that is how they will be presented – the actions of a few may cause the public to see angling in a different light. Over time, and it may be a long time, our sport may well come to be seen not as some gentle and mildly dotty pursuit, but as a grubby and catchpenny business in which all sense of fair play has been abandoned and in which our quarry is cynically and cruelly abused.

There are likely to be other effects.

One is that over time, the excesses of some will lead to a dulling of sensibilities and a lowering of the acceptance threshold within the sport: 'if they are already doing that, or have been doing the other long enough, then maybe this is not so bad or has anyway become necessary.' The necessity to institutionalise records for hand-reared fish, which have nothing to do with record fish as they have always been accepted and everything to do with greed and the prowess of the fish-farmer, may be seen as a case in point.

Another side-effect is that we could see perhaps our greatest strength – our numbers – decline. The morality of angling, as of any other field sport, is not all black and white. At a time when the earth increasingly is seen as a fragile place, one shared by all the creatures on it, we could see the commitment of some within the sport gradually weakening in the face of trends they find unacceptable. More seriously, we could fail to attract young recruits to the extent that we have in the past.

I do not for a moment suggest that all of this is about to happen overnight or even within the lifetime of my own generation. But we do not have to look far to see how rapidly events can move and how seemingly immutable reference points can vanish without trace.

For all the wonderful satisfactions of our sport and for all its huge popularity, nothing at all can be taken for granted. Right now, excesses within angling are gradually inching us in one direction when public opinion is moving in the other. Only by resisting all excesses will we avoid a premature collision – no matter how far away that collision might be.

Tackle by Post

The growth of direct-mail tackle sales has been an interesting development. At the end of the twentieth century, it seems, an approaching trout season is marked less by icicles melting and snowdrops opening, than by the crash and crump of catalogues landing in the hall.

Most of these catalogues come from home-grown suppliers, a few from suppliers overseas, a small handful from foreign companies, mostly American, that have set up shop over here. I found myself on the mailing list of one company in no time. FROM *The Times*, December 29, 1993.

A thoughtful American supplier of fishing tackle and accessories, now established in this country, has taken to sending me his sales catalogues. They are things of wonder. They illustrate a range of products that would fill several warehouses and have been compiled by someone whose stock of adjectives would fill several more.

Words like 'rugged' and 'durable', 'lightweight' and 'unique' are everywhere. Superlatives abound. Many items, I am impressed to see, are 'World's Best', a claim that must have required so much conscientious research and travel, such scrutiny of patents and testings in the field, that one marvels the brochures got published at all.

Little expense has been spared in producing them. They are printed on glossy paper, are neatly laid out and the captions are very nearly as colourful as the photographs. The products themselves are in the main very good. All of which makes it surprising that so curious a mistake should continue to creep in.

I refer, of course, to the fishing waistcoats. The waistcoats shown cannot possibly be to scale. They look like ordinary waistcoats that might be worn by ordinary fly fishermen, yet any waistcoat carrying even half the items the catalogues suggest are 'essential', could only be stood up in by a weightlifter adapting the press-and-lift technique.

Even unladen and of regular size, these waistcoats must be garments of substance. They have pockets that have been built in for putting things into and attachments that have been added for attaching things to.

There are fabric pockets, nylon pockets, transparent plastic pockets, mesh pockets. There are velcro flaps, zip fasteners, press-studs and buttons. There are loops for holding the rod so that the hands can be kept free, metal rings for clipping collapsible landing nets to, scores of little places where spring-loaded zingy things with retractable cords can be attached, for attaching other things to – some of them, no doubt, likewise spring-laden. One memorable model has pockets both front and back, the rear pockets being reached by unzipping the garment at either side and rotating it, rather in the manner of a fairground roundabout. None of this is to suggest, of course, that all of these pockets and appendages are unnecessary: indeed, no. Every last pocket and appendage is necessary because of all that must be carried.

I speak here not only of the waterproofed knot-tying guide which the catalogue advertises, an 'instant streamside reference' for tying basic fishing knots (and where better, indeed, to practise knot-tying than on the banks of an expensive chalkstream with the trout rising merrily all around?). No, what I have in mind are the Non-Glare Super Forceps, the fisherman's multipurpose tool with the black nickel oxide finish that 'looks nice on your waistcoat and won't scare fish because of reflections'; the Premium zingy thing with its 'rugged, stainless housing and clip that won't corrode'; the Never-Miss Strike Indicators to assist those who cannot see or react to the yank of a taking fish – perhaps because their sweater sleeves are held fast to their waistcoats, caught on some velcro flap.

Naturally, in this plethora of desirable and essential kit, there have to be priorities and I am relieved the catalogue gives safety and survival a responsibly high place.

For those rugged folk preparing to explore alone the River Itchen near Winchester, the catalogue has the Thermometer/ Compass Zipper Pull, a device that will attach to the tag on a waistcoat zip and comes with the so-easily forgotten Wind Chill Chart on the back. For those beating their way upriver to Stratford-on-Avon – 'don't be caught wet and cold without a way to start a life-saving fire' – the catalogue offers a waterproof lighter housed in a brushed and I can only presume rugged aluminium case. For anyone cut off from civilisation in the sparsely-populated mid-Thames Valley there is a stainless steel and leather Sloe Gin Set with which to do barter with the natives.

Not everything in this catalogue is a matter of life and death, of course. Some things are more important than either. I do not, of course, refer to trivia like rods and reels and lines and places to go fishing. I mean seriously important things. Things like, for example, the World's Finest Kneeboot 'for those who spend a lot of time in their Kneeboots', and which are so cunningly designed that they make 'on and off operations a dream'. I am talking about the Fly Fisherman's Tool, the essential nature and vital functions of which I need not dwell upon. I am talking about the Head Net Hat, complete with its over-the-shoulder mesh for keeping midges at bay and which 'wads up into practically no space' (just like the one tastefully modelled).

Over the various editions of this catalogue, items have moved in and items have moved out. I regret the disappearance of the World's Finest Tackle Bag, 'hand-crafted and appointed in Latigo leather', which came complete with its solid oak accessory drawer and which costs – thanks, no doubt, to merciless cost-cutting and the shaving of margins – a trifling £250. I am pleased to welcome back the Portable Wellington Wardrobe with its 'practical' – and goodness knows, us fishermen need to be prac-tical – non-rusting fastener.

I could go on and on and possibly have. But there is surely no need to say more to justify my position, which is that I plan to buy the lot.

I may end up tripping over and tangling my rods and nets, and be so festooned with zingy things, and things hanging from zingy things, that they bounce and jostle around me like corks on a swagman's hat; but at least I'll have all the essentials and a companion on the riverbank.

He will be the person wearing my back-up waistcoat and carrying my other tackle bag. His conversation may not be too hot, but you can't have everything. All weightlifters have ever done is grunt.

A Tucked-away Eddy

The fly fisher in a boat may have a friend alongside him, the match angler on the bank may have hundreds of others all around; but when a fish rises or a float dips and sidles, all else dissolves. Concentration cocoons. The still centre of angling is a solitary place.

Even so, us anglers are gregarious folk. The fishing club is the oldest of our institutions, not only because it can make fishing cheaper and access to water easier. We want our still moments but we seek out companionship, too.

Clubs can be of all kinds and sizes. They can be founded on all kinds of principles, with all kinds of aims and have any manner of conventions. I was once invited to speak to a club – a very successful club – that was unusual in almost every clublike respect. It had, I discovered, been founded by a remarkable man whose place in angling has been largely forgotten. It was, of course, in Yorkshire – that foreign land. FROM *The Times*, May 19, 1992.

For the first time in many years, April saw me on a North-country river and opening my account with fish taken on the downstream wet fly.

The river was one of the most beautiful in England – the Ure, which winds and glides and rumples its way through the grey-walled fastnesses of Wensleydale. The occasion proved especially appropriate: the 100th anniversary of the founding of the Tanfield Angling Club.

The name of the Tanfield Angling Club is not one that is normally on the mind; one that couples naturally with that of, say, the Houghton or the Piscatorials, or any other in the handful of illustrious centenarians in the angling world. Yet it is there among them and, although it may be scarcely known on the national scene, it is an extraordinary club that has a fascinating historical background.

The reasons why individual fishing clubs reach a great age, the qualities that make them special, naturally vary from one to another. However, it is especially easy to list the things that have not contributed to this tiny club's longevity and that have given it a waiting list as long as a roach-fisher's pole.

One thing that has not contributed has been the club's social life. The centenary dinner, at which I was privileged to speak, was the first social event of any kind in the club's entire history and one dinner in a 100 years – say 10 in 1,000 – does not rank as Bacchanalian self-indulgence, even in Yorkshire.

Another thing that has not contributed has been the splendour or convenience of the club's premises, because it has none. Nor even has it been the tie which binds, because the club has no tie.

Indeed, the club has none of the outward manifestations of success and self-declaration that many other, seemingly more privileged and much shorter-lived institutions, have held to be essential.

What the Tanfield Angling Club has concentrated upon – and concentrated upon wonderfully well – has been the quality of its waters and the maintenance of them, in every sense.

The club's waters extend over several miles of the Ure, mainly upstream of West Tanfield bridge. They were chosen 100 years ago with the most expert eye and include not only some of the finest wet-fly water I have ever fished but some of the finest dry-fly water, too.

The most literal way that the club has maintained its waters has been by fostering good relations with its riparian owners and the owners have remained supportive and involved, from day one. The club has always had its own, dedicated keepers – indeed, for the greater part of the 100 years it has drawn its keepers from three generations of the same fishing family, the

Sturdys – and it was the first Sturdy, Tom, who designed the famous 'Sturdy's Fancy'.

The club has run its own hatchery from the outset and has ensured that the water is always sensibly stocked. The club has ensured that its members are able to enjoy the water by having rules that are not overly restrictive and that, for the most part, rely on commonsense and goodwill in their application.

However, perhaps the most important thing the club did to ensure its long-term soundness was to choose the right founder. And that, to my surprise, turned out to be the remarkable Francis Maximilian Walbran.

Other than among those who take an interest in such things, the name of Walbran will mean little. Yet Francis Walbran, who owned a tackle shop in Leeds, was one of the great anglers of his time and the man who, perhaps more than any other, provided the living bridge between the North-country and the South-country schools of fly fishing at the time of their most intensive development.

Fly fishing in the latter half of the 19th century was a ferment of creativity. In the North, Michael Theakston, of Ripon, produced *A List of Natural Flies*, John Jackson, of Tanfield itself, produced *The Practical Flyfisher* and T.E. Pritt published his famous *Yorkshire Trout Flies*, all of them moving the great art forward. In the South the monumental works of Frederic Halford – and especially his *Dry Fly Fishing in Theory and Practice* – codified the art of dry fly fishing as it is now exercised all over the world.

Walbran, a well-known angling correspondent – he wrote for *The Northern Angler* and the *Fishing Gazette* – and an author in his own right, bestrode both schools and fished with the greatest anglers of the day in each, among them Pritt, R.B. Marston (founder of The Flyfishers' Club of London, of which Walbran was a member), Francis Francis, G.S. Marryat and Halford himself. Walbran was even invited by Halford – long reviled as a purist by those who have never read what he wrote – to fish the Test for grayling with a worm.

It seems likely that Walbran's South-country friends, several of whom fished the waters around Houghton, were influences on Walbran when the criteria for the Tanfield club were drawn up.

Certainly it was Walbran who took all the initiatives. It was Walbran who tested out local sentiment on the founding of such a club; Walbran who found the club's magnificent waters; Walbran who called the inaugural meeting; Walbran who moved so quickly that within three weeks the club was appointing its first keeper; Walbran who was instrumental in seeing that the club established a hatchery before even that first year was out. Walbran's club even adopted its own answer to the Houghton's Grosvenor Hotel – the Bruce Arms, at West Tanfield, a splendid hostelry to which Walbran and his friends frequently repaired and in which I have myself spent the ends of several happy days passed on the club's water.

The extent of the club's – and North-country angling's – indebtedness to Walbran can be seen in the churchyard at West Tanfield. Walbran was drowned on February 15, 1909, while fishing just downstream of the road bridge only a short cast away and a beautifully carved headstone depicting creel, fish, net and rods, was raised over his grave by public subscription.

Notable and moving though that monument is, Francis Walbran was the kind of man who would undoubtedly have regarded the centenary celebrations of the club he founded, as a greater memorial.

On the broad stream of a century's fly fishing, the vast majority of angling clubs come and go like so many passing eddies. Few prove lasting features. The tiny, tucked-away club at Tanfield has been such a feature: and like many a tucked-away eddy it has proved, upon exploration, to hold at least one remarkable fish.

Last Cast

It is easier to describe the fishing experience than to say what fishing means, even for ourselves. There is just so much going on inside that we cannot resolve or touch. What follows is a description of one experience of my own which happens to say a little, I think, about what fishing means to me. I do not remember consciously writing it that way, but that is its result.

The essay raises a dilemma – to kill or not to kill – that will be familiar to many anglers. I have not always felt the equanimity and elation recorded here, on resolving it for the one instance described. By the same token, there have been many more times when I have felt in no dilemma at all. It seems a suitably ambivalent point on which to end.

FROM *The Flyfishers*, the Centenary Book of the Flyfishers' Club, 1984.

It's late August and I'm on the river.

Just downstream, for half a century and more, Mr Skues studied the ways of a trout with his fly, imitated the nymph and pushed the cause of the thinking fly fisher a light-year ahead. A little way upstream Lord Grey kept his beat. Halford fished here, too; and so did Marryat and Francis and Marston and the rest.

Very little can have changed in the years in between. The same flowing crystal slides the same course through the same timeless meadows. Along the valley floor, just as they always did, cattle drowse and acquiesce their lives away; and here and there young mares, poised as ballerinas, arch elegant necks down and nibble their way slowly across the paddocks without pause to look up.

As before, long tails swish idly behind them, elegantly as any fly-rod was ever made to move.

It's evening.

Downstream, where the sun sets, the water is turning to liquid gold and the air is filled with that hot-day, high-summer hallucinatory haze, distancing the far bank, stilling time. All around me the mute semaphores of the duns are lifting; water-voles are bustling their secret, sharp-eyed, sniffle-snuffing errands along tussocky margins; and rings oil out.

For long moments I steep myself in it before wrenching myself around to take stock.

I'm on the very lip of the river, which burbles by a few inches from my toes, funnelled hard into the bank by the island. A thick belt of sedges, seven feet high and more, hems me in from behind and to my left, close enough to touch, a young willow trails her finger-tips in the water and dreamily explores her reflection. Between them and the place where the bank falls away I've about eight feet by two feet in which to move. It will have to do.

Fifteen yards upstream, where the island is widest, the river narrows even further, squeezing and rumpling its way past the dense bed of crowfoot where he lives.

I first saw him in the early afternoon, his tail fanning the cushion of water which the emerald raft holds back. From immediately behind he'd looked strangely foreshortened. Only the dark bulk of his shoulder prompted me not to cast at once; to watch as he drifted compactly from side to side, riding the water like some great tethered kite. And then he saw, late and far off, something he wanted. He jack-knifed around, sharp-edged and predatory, and for the first time showed his full length. Moments later, he disappeared without giving me a chance.

Tonight, with the sun going down and with the heat we've had, I know he'll show again, I can feel it in my bones. I clear away the twigs and the debris where my line might fall, make myself comfortable and wait. Time passes. I am totally alone. There is only the vignette of the weedbed and the water around it. The great trout and I are cocooned.

After a while – I don't know how long – he comes. The

reflections in front of the weedbed stir, and the dark bob of his neb breaks the surface. It is a subliminal movement, so soft and brief that most times I'd have missed it or have noticed only the full-stop winking out.

I shuffle softly, easing the tension which seizes my sinews and settle myself again. I want to be absolutely confident before I decide on the fly, the cast, anything.

It's as well that I do. After a few more lilts to the surface his behaviour changes. Half out of the water he suddenly comes with a whoopee, Bunteresque, lolloping lunge, teased up by a brown piece of carpet fluff which flutters broadside to the current and trickles a thin V behind it.

A few more joyous surgings and all guesswork is removed, all hesitation gone. I put up a sedge, crouch cautiously forward and wriggle the end of the fly-line clear of my top-ring. I'm ready when he is.

Half a minute later and I'm casting. I'm too confined to make it elegant: there's no wristy stylishness to propel the line back, no surgical cut forward for the *coup de grace*: it's an awkward, aerialised pleading and bartering with the soft evening airs and faint pluck-plucking of the tall sedges behind.

But it all goes right. The line stays clear on the backcast and lengthens silkily ahead. For a brief instant I glimpse the fly descending, floating down through the last, water-colour wash of the evening light. And then lose it.

Nothing happens. My left hand nibbles in line, I lift off and throw awkwardly again. This time he comes at once, almost taking me by surprise with his surging, half-breasting of the water, powerful and compelling, remote and unconnected with me, both at the same time; like a street drama viewed from some high-storey window.

When I tighten, left hand down, right hand up, he does exactly what I knew he'd do. For a few dreadful moments he makes it, the weed rolling heavily at the surface, the rod wrenched around to wincing point, the leader, all elasticity taken up, singing like piano wire, twing, twang, oriental ting-tong. Then, urged by the pressure on his own desperate movements he finds he's backed himself out and races towards me.

I don't suppose the battle really lasts long – in truth it never does. Three minutes, perhaps; maybe four: but they're long minutes as they always are, incrementally compiled from used-up, milked-out seconds, each one recorded by the thump of my heart.

Suddenly, it's over. For the last time I persuade him away from the willow, lead him head-up into the stream with his tail wafting behind him and then simply back him down into the net I've got ready. He can know nothing about it until I lift, he feels suddenly crushed by his own weight in the air and his eyes can't see any more.

On the ground he's too spent to protest: he simply lies gasping in the shroud of the net, gleaming, clean, vibrant and silver, powerful and magnetic. And big, extraordinarily big.

Then it begins, the debate; tiny voices somewhere inside, wheedling, cajoling, sternly reproachful. And then wheedling again and probing.

'What a fish – what a *magnificent* fish! He'll cause a stir back at the hut! . . . Stir? Stir? What stir? You can't kill a fish like this. He's got to go back, he's got to . . . But you *do* want to keep him, don't you? You do want to show him off. And you haven't taken a fish for weeks.'

And so it goes, backwards and forwards, forwards and back ... 'And only yesterday the keeper asked you to put a few in the book ...'

I despair of myself. Even while the debate's going on and my left hand registers the life beneath it, my right hand is insinuating itself into a pocket, groping and tracing among the bottles and spools, seeking out the smoothness of the priest; closing around it.

I bring it down twice – once to do the job, the second time to make sure. I can see nothing of the light that crashes through his brain, or the black consuming darkness that rolls up behind it; but there's no escaping that they're there. His whole body trembles and his tail, to the left of my hand where I hold him, arches up, quivers electrified for a long moment and then slowly subsides, laying itself gently out on the ground, fretting a little, arranging itself, succumbing. Then nothing.

And then, all at once, the seal around me cracks and the rest of the world floods in. I can hear the river again and a dog in the distance and notice with some surprise that a car on the road has its sidelights on.

Suddenly I realise how dark it is, how long I must have been here and a briskness takes over. I wash my hands in the river, nip the fly from my leader and reel in. Then I pick up my net, slip my fingers through the trout's gills and stride off into the dusk, the heavy thwack-thwack of his body on my leg as I go.

It's not a long walk back, but by the time I turn away through the woods and leave the darkening river behind there is inside me an immense stillness, an unfathomed calm. Once again my rod and my line, the river and the fish, the light and the sounds and my need have taken me into that world which all fly fishers know; have carried me down again into those soft-stirring womb-waters, dimly remembered.

Once again by the time I reach the clearing and break down my rod I know that spiritually, philosophically, temperamentally I have somehow 'been home'. And that I have returned, for however briefly, renewed.